THE TRUTH BEHIND REAL SUCCESS

The Truth Behind Real Success
by Robynn K. Coates

Printed in the United States of America

ISBN 9781619969445

www.xulonpress.com

Don't look for shortcuts to God. The market is flooded with surefire, easygoing formulas for a successful life that can be practiced in your spare time. Don't fall for that stuff, even though crowds of people do. The way to life—to God!—is vigorous and requires total attention.

Matthew 7:13-14, MSG

Contents

INTRODUCTION

For what shall it profit a man, if he shall gain the whole world, and lose his own soul?
Mark 8:36, KJV

As I was in the midst of writing this book, I turned on the news and saw it reported that a top executive of a financial institution had committed suicide. The news station flashed aerial pictures of his enormous house on their newscast. To most, he appeared to have had it all: the position, the money, the house, the family, and the material possessions. But was this really success?

What is true success? We can make up our own definition or subscribe to the definition of our culture and society, but if these definitions don't align with principles, they are shallow and meaningless. This book takes a look at not only some of these life-governing principles, but also the source of these principles: Jesus Christ. He gave us the real definition of success in the example He left for us—fulfilling the purpose for which He was sent—to set the captive free and redeem mankind from its sinful state. We can see the purpose God has for us in Ephesians 2:10:

For we are God's handiwork, created in Christ Jesus to do good works, which God prepared in advance for us to do.

As a former teacher, I like to use analogies to help illustrate a point. So imagine this: You are standing in front of your dream car. It is everything you could hope and dream for. Now imagine you were given the keys to this vehicle and told it belongs to you. Excitedly you get inside and turn the key. However, to your disappointment, the car won't start, and nothing you do can get it running.

If it was determined that the car would never run, but it was yours to keep, would you consider the vehicle a success? The obvious answer is no, because it did not fulfill its purpose. Sure, it looked good. It even had all the bells and whistles you dreamed of, but ultimately it didn't deliver on what it was created for and what it was designed to do.

That picture describes what our lives look like if we have a whole lot of "stuff," that is, material possessions and achievements, but have not fulfilled our purpose. It's what the Bible talks about in the verse listed at the beginning of this introduction: gaining the world, but losing our souls.

My mission in writing this book is to help people fulfill their purpose. I pray the principles contained in these pages will encourage and inspire you to pursue the highest calling in your life—fulfilling your God-given destiny. In my pursuit of knowing Christ and walking in His freedom, I have learned these lessons. And they have changed my life.

Before you read this book, let me make a couple of suggestions. Instead of reading it just as a book, use it as a journal as well. At the end of each chapter, you will find a question or activity for you to do that will help you focus on a principle you may want to work on or implement in your life. If it helps, use the pages to jot down your answers. I began reading books this way, and my reading experience has been enriched as a result. I now mark up my books with highlighters and write pencil and pen markings in the margin. My scribbles help make a point jump off the page and become a reality in my life. This works for me. Maybe it will work for you as well.

My prayer for you is James 1:22:

Do not merely listen to the word, and so deceive yourselves. Do what it says.

May your life be an example to others of what true success really is.

1.)

THE TWO DEAL BREAKERS

Be strong and very courageous. Be careful to obey all the law my servant Moses gave you; do not turn from it to the right or to the left, that you may be successful wherever you go.
Joshua 1:7

All throughout the Bible, you can see that God wants you to succeed. He's got an awesome plan for you, and carefully following His plan *always* leads to success. But as humans, we like to come up with our own plans for success. We want to define success by our terms and not necessarily by God's.

The Bible tells us in Isaiah 55 that not only are our ways not God's ways, but God's ways are higher than our ways. God's imaginations and thoughts towards us are obviously far greater than what we could ever conceive. Ephesians 3:20 says:

Now to him who is able to do immeasurably more than all we ask or imagine, according to his power that is at work within us.

In your mind, what would be the greatest accomplishment you could achieve? The best-case scenario? Guess what? God's thoughts about you are higher and better than your wildest imagination. You will never be able to outdo Him.

So if this is God's plan and His desire for us, why isn't everyone living a victorious and successful life? Although God has made a successful life available to us, it isn't guaranteed. God has some guidelines that must be followed in order to partake of this abundant living. These guidelines are found in God's "Success Manual of Life"—the Bible.

We are all familiar with the instructor's manual that comes with a new product. This manual describes how our new gadget works. The manual is made by the company that created the product because, after all, they are the ones who know the product the best. Not only are they the most qualified to give advice and input on the product, but they are also the authority on that particular item.

The awesome thing is that in life we are not left on our own to try to figure out how to live. Instead, our creator has given us a manual to help us maneuver through life. He knows us best because He designed and created us. Following His directions will ultimately lead us to success and fulfilling the purpose He created us for.

Unfortunately, there are deal breakers that will prevent us from enjoying the good life that God has made possible through His Word, the Bible. These deal breakers will prevent us from partaking of all that God has made available to us.

Deal Breaker #1—Not Being Part of the Family

This shouldn't be hard for us to understand. My children have free access to my stuff. They eat freely from my husband's and my refrigerator and pantry. They play all throughout our house without any sense of hesitation. They help themselves freely to our provisions and are completely taken care of and provided for by us. The neighborhood kids do not have this same luxury.

Becoming part of God's family is what is referred to as being a "Christian" or a "believer," being "in Christ," being "saved," or being what John 3:3 refers to as "born again."

We read in Ephesians 1:5:

He predestined us to be adopted as his sons through Jesus Christ, in accordance with his pleasure and will. (NIV 1984)

How is a person adopted as a child into God's family? The process is a simple one. Romans 10:9–10 gives us the two necessary steps:

That if you confess with your mouth, "Jesus is Lord," and believe in your heart that God raised him from the dead, you will be saved. (NIV 1984)

The moment you say this prayer, you become part of the family. From here you begin the journey of becoming Christlike. You begin this endeavor by spending time daily in God's Word, the Bible. Here you will begin to see how God thinks. You will learn what pleases Him and how to live. In addition to reading God's Word, you will want to spend time in prayer. This simply means that you talk to God and then listen for Him to talk to you.

Deal Breaker #2—Not Obeying God's Word

God's Word is full of promises. And His promises are really, really good! He promises that He will open His treasury to you and pour out blessings so great you won't have room enough to contain them (see Deuteronomy 28, Malachi 3). He promises that He will bless *all* the work of your hands and will make it prosper. Take a look for yourself and you will find some pretty awesome stuff contained within the pages of your Bible.

However, these promises come with a condition, and that condition is obedience. Obedience always pays dividends. Unfortunately, those dividends aren't always seen immediately, and because of this, it is our human nature to want to take shortcuts and get immediate gratification. The alternative to obedience is sin, and, let's face it, sin is fun. If it weren't fun, we wouldn't be tempted to participate. The Bible even says that sin is pleasurable—*but* only for a season. Its end result is always death.

Death can occur on many levels. We typically think of physical death, but did you know that you can experience death in your relationships, finances, and marriage, as well as in every other aspect of your life? Failure to obey God in these areas always results in death.

It would be nice if the consequences of sin were immediate, like a shock collar or the pain you experience when you burn your hand on a hot object. The learning curve on such experiences is steep. However, because we don't immediately see the ill effects of sin, we are deceived into believing that sin has no consequence except for the pleasure that it initially brings. Then, when we begin to suffer the consequences, we don't pin them on our previous choices. Instead, we choose to blame God. Proverbs 19:3 says:

> ***A man's own folly ruins his life, yet his heart rages against the Lord.*** (NIV 1984)

Are you blaming God for things that are simply the product of choices you have made? We will talk more about this in chapter 18, but for now, ask yourself this question: "Have I been making poor choices, and am I unsatisfied with the fruit that is being produced in my life?" If you answered yes to that question, take heart! Today can be a new beginning for you. If you have not made Jesus the Lord of your life, today is the day of salvation! If you have at one time given your life to Christ but are not living a totally surrendered life, you can change that right now. First John 1:9 says:

If we confess our sins, he is faithful and just and will forgive us our sins and purify us from all unrighteousness.

You can have a fresh, clean start right now. Don't wait another day to embark upon the successful life that God has for you.

1. Where do you stand with God today? ______________________
____
____
____

2. Is there a deal breaker standing in the way of your living the life God destined for you to live?
____
____
____

2.)

WHO ARE YOU?

And because you belong to Christ you are complete, having everything you need.
Colossians 2:10, ERV

When it comes to walking a victorious and successful Christian life, do you ever feel as though you're a kid on the outside looking in at all the other kids enjoying the playground with its many amenities? You earnestly desire to be in on the fun, enjoying the thrill and excitement of the playground experience, but for some reason, it seems just out of your grasp. Your experience just doesn't seem to match the instruction given in the Bible, and as a result, your life seems to be one of meager existence.

Do you feel distant from God? Do you struggle with sin even though you know that God has made a way for you to be free from it? In his book *Victory Over The Darkness*, Neil T. Anderson says:

If we really knew God, our behavior would change radically and instantly. That's what happened in Scripture. Whenever heaven opened to reveal the glory of God, individual witnesses were immediately and profoundly changed. I believe that the greatest determinant of mental and spiritual health and freedom is a true understanding of God and a right relationship with Him. A good theology is an indispensable prerequisite to a good psychology.[1]

What does it mean to really know God? Look at what the apostle Paul had to say about knowing God in Philippians 3:10:

[For my determined purpose is] that I may know Him [that I may progressively become more deeply and intimately acquainted with Him, perceiving and recognizing and understanding the wonders of His Person more strongly and more clearly. (AMP)

Moses prayed a similar prayer in Exodus 33:13:

Now therefore I pray you, if I have found favor in Your sight, show me now Your way, that I may know You [progressively become more deeply and intimately acquainted with You, perceiving and recognizing and understanding more strongly and clearly] and that I may find favor in Your sight. (AMP)

The good news of the gospel is that, yes, God does want you to know Him. Not only does He want you to know Him, but He has also made a way for you to know Him. That way is His son, Jesus Christ.

The message of the gospel is so incredibly profound, but it is also so simple. It all started when Adam and Eve in their perfect state disobeyed God. Suddenly their perfect world was shattered. The harmonious fellowship they had known with God came to an abrupt halt. A chasm then existed, and man was separated from God. Sin always has this effect. It isolates and leaves us totally destitute. Man then had to find a different way to relate to God. For thousands of years following, we see man trying desperately to redeem himself from the terrible mistake made by Adam and Eve.

No matter how hard man tried, his efforts were in vain. He needed a Savior. That Savior was Jesus Christ. He was born to a virgin, the Son of Man and the Son of God. He was perfect. In fact, he is called the perfect Lamb of God. Before Jesus died, the law required man to deal with his sin by offering a sacrifice. This sacrifice was an animal without spot or blemish. Symbolically, the sin of man was then passed on to the animal. Although the sacrifice allowed man to deal with his sin momentarily, it had to be repeated each time man sinned. It was imperfect. A new and better way was needed.

The old law worked on man from the outside in. But when Jesus died and rose from the dead, the sacrifice for sin was made once and for all. Jesus was the perfect Lamb of God. He was the sacrifice that took away our sins. Man could now be made right with God and have a new heart. By going to the cross, Jesus made it possible for man to be changed from the inside out.

This is the incredible story of redemption. Once you experience this incredible transformation, it doesn't stop here. This is only the beginning. Your heart has been changed once and for all. This is called justification. However, once justification occurs, then it is time for you to be changed in your attitudes, actions, words, and thoughts. This process is called sanctification. Many believers stop at justification and never really venture down the path of sanctification. This is unfortunate, because this is where true freedom and success are found. This is where you begin to grow into maturity and fulfill your purpose.

I believe that this failure to pursue sanctification occurs largely because believers lack knowledge of their true identity. What I mean by this is that they don't understand what qualities they possess as children of God, as well as the provisions God has made available to them. They simply do not know who they are in Christ. And when people don't understand who they are in Christ, their lives will be riddled with frustration, failure, and disappointment.

Let me share with you a partial list of how God looks at you once you put your faith in Jesus Christ.

In Christ:

- ***You are a new creation. The old has gone; behold, all things have become new*** (2 Cor. 5:17).
- ***You are set free from sin and become a slave to righteousness*** (Rom. 6:18).
- ***You can do all things through Christ who strengthens you*** (Phil. 4:13).
- ***You are God's handiwork, born anew to do good works*** (Eph 2:10).
- ***You have not been given the spirit of fear, but the spirit of power, love, and self-discipline*** (2 Tim. 1:7).
- ***You have a friend (Jesus) who will never leave you nor forsake you*** (Heb. 13:5).
- ***You have a new heart that desires to walk in God's ways*** (Ezek. 36:26–27).

- ***You have the Holy Spirit, who is your comforter, helper, strengthener, and teacher*** (John 14:26).
- ***You have God's peace*** (John 14:27; 16:33; Phil. 4:7).
- ***You are an overcomer because greater is He that is in you than he that is in the world*** (1 John 4:4).
- ***You have access to God*** (Eph. 3:12).
- ***You are a saint*** (Eph 2:19).

Wow! What a list. And it is only a partial one. If you are a believer, these statements are true of you. The only qualifier is being "in Christ." Sadly, many believers think that they are wretched old sinners, and as a result, that is what their life reflects: defeat and failure. But regardless of how poorly you may be performing or how unworthy you may feel, it doesn't nullify the truth of God's Word.

"So what do I do about these truths?" you may ask. There is nothing for you to do but to believe them and accept them as truth. One key way to accept them as truth is to confess them with your mouth.

Being in Christ comes with tremendous benefits. God's plan is for you to know Him. Could there be anything better?

In what areas in your life do you feel as though you are lacking God's truth? The best way to attack a lie is with the truth. Identify the areas in your life where you are falling for the devil's lie and then counteract those lies with the truth of God's Word. Here's an example:

Lie: I am a loser and can't do anything right.

Truth: ***I am fearfully and wonderfully made*** (Ps. 139:14). ***I can do all this through him who gives me strength*** (Phil. 4:13).

As you begin to challenge the lies that have dominated your life with the truth of God's Word, freedom and maturity will begin to emerge. Truth is what sets you free (John 8:32).

So what are you waiting for? You don't have to be standing on the outside looking in at the freedom that only God can give. It's available to you today. Will you come in and partake?

You can begin today to replace the lies that hold you captive with God's truth that will set you free.

- Make a list of all the lies you are believing and then counteract those lies with the truth of God's Word. ______________________________
____
____
____

- Then begin thinking about and saying those truths daily (this is called meditating). As you begin to do so, it will change your life. You will begin to fulfill your purpose and live the life God created you to live.

3.)

GOING AROUND IN CIRCLES

It is [only] eleven days' journey from Horeb by the way of Mount Seir to Kadesh- barnea [on Canaan's border; yet Israel took forty years to get beyond it].
Deuteronomy 1:2, AMP

Do you ever feel as though your journey towards your dream is taking you a lot longer than what it should actually take? Maybe, like me, you had a goal of losing some weight, but what should have taken four or five months took years. In my case, it took over twenty years. Wowza!

We see that the Israelites were no different. Imagine taking off for the Promised Land, knowing you should arrive at your destination in less than two weeks, but instead going around in circles for forty years! And even then, most of those Israelites who began the journey were not allowed to complete the trip because of their unbelieving hearts.

It can be frustrating when we aren't making the progress we know we should be making. Even God may be telling us to start moving forward. After spending forty years in the desert, Moses went to the people and said:

The Lord our God said to us in Horeb, you have dwelt long enough on this mountain.
Deuteronomy 1:6, AMP

What destination have you set out for that you should have arrived at maybe weeks, months, or even years ago? God is not only telling you that you have dwelt long enough on your mountain, but He is also extending His grace and His power to help you to get past the mountain in your life and move into Canaan, your promised land. Canaan, in the Old Testament, is a representation of God's promises. It represents the abundant life God has made available to you, free from bondage.

Are you ready to get past your mountain and walk in God's promises and His freedom? Not only did God tell the Israelites to get past their mountain, He also told them how to do it. We'll take a look at this instruction in the next chapter. For now, let me leave you with a question: what mountain have you dwelt on long enough?

Take a moment to think and pray about the mountain in your life that God is telling you to cross. If there are more than one, list them all, from the seemingly small ones to those that seem insurmountable. ___________

____

____

____

____

Then realize that God never asks you to do something that He won't give you the grace to do!

4.)

THE SUCCESS FORMULA

This Book of the Law shall not depart out of your mouth, but you shall meditate on it day and night, that you may observe and do according to all that is written in it. For then you shall make your way prosperous, and then you shall deal wisely and have good success.
Joshua 1:8, AMP

We don't often hear the word *meditate* in our society. When we do, many times we may associate it with some Eastern religious practice that involves clearing the mind of thoughts while in a sitting position, legs crossed and eyes closed. But this is not the picture of meditation we get from the Bible. Joshua 1:8 gives us the Bible's application of the word *meditate.*

MEDITATION ON GOD'S WORD + OBEDIENCE TO THE WORD = SUCCESS

The Hebrew words for *meditation* mean ***"to sigh or murmur"*** and ***"to muse or rehearse in one's mind"*** [2] (Wikipedia). *To meditate* means we take a thought and ponder it, looking at all sides as well as considering its relevance for everyday living. When the Bible talks about meditation, it refers to a practice done not only in a quiet place of solitude, but also in the hustle and bustle of the day. Meditation can be done when you're driving, cooking, walking to the water cooler for a quick break, or in numerous other activities. In fact, the Bible instructs us to meditate day and night. Psalm 1:2 says:

But his delight and desire are in the law of the Lord, and on His law (the precepts, the instructions, the teachings of God) he habitually meditates (ponders and studies) by day and by night. (AMP)

Does meditation mean that you are thinking about the Bible all day long and place no value on giving thought to your daily tasks? Not at all. In fact, we are to give ourselves wholly to the task God has given us. I love what Jim Elliot, a missionary to the tribes of Ecuador, had to say about the subject. His advice on living in the moment was this: "Wherever you are, be all there." We are to be fully committed to what we are working on at the moment, and we need to be fully engaged in what God has assigned us to do, regardless of how mundane the task may seem. There are times when we won't be thinking directly on God's Word, but a meditating heart will be attuned to God's ways and His thoughts. A meditating heart will also find itself in praise and adoration of God and His goodness.

There are many benefits of meditating on God's Word. One of those benefits is that meditation leads us to obedience. The psalmist David said:

I have hidden your word in my heart that I might not sin against you. Psalm 119:11

If you find yourself having difficulty obeying God in a certain area of your life, begin to meditate on scriptures regarding that subject. For example, if you are having a challenge controlling your tongue and not engaging in gossip and speech that is displeasing to God, find out what the Bible says about the subject.

- ***"Do not let any unwholesome talk come out of your mouths, but only what is helpful for building others up according to their needs, that it may benefit those who listen"*** (Ephesians 4:29).
- ***"For whoever would love life and see good days must keep their tongue from evil and their lips from deceitful speech"*** (1 Peter 3:10).

There are many more scriptures on the subject, and you may want to look at all of them. Then begin to meditate on the scriptures that really speak to you. When you do, you are setting into motion a spiritual principle of reaping what you sow.

Once we begin to obey God's Word, the natural consequence is success. Now there are many definitions of success, but taking our cues from the Bible, true success is knowing God and fulfilling the purpose He has created us for. This is where true peace and contentment are found. This is true success.

I think that many people view Christians as narrow minded, weak, and defeated. If you asked them the first thing that came to mind when they heard the word *Christian*, they probably wouldn't use the word *successful*. But is this how the Bible paints the picture of the believer?

- Romans 8:37 says, ***"No, in all these things we are more than conquerors through him who loved us."***
- Philippians 4:13 says, ***"I can do all this through him who gives me strength."***
- Second Corinthians 2:14 says, ***"But thanks be to God who always leads us in triumphal procession in Christ"*** (NIV 1984).
- Deuteronomy 28:13 says, ***"The Lord will make you the head, not the tail. If you pay attention to the commands of the Lord your God that I give you this day and carefully follow them, you will always be at the top, never at the bottom."***

Is that the picture of a defeated person?

One thing we have to understand is that God doesn't lead us down paths that are unfruitful, unproductive, and full of failure. It's just not God's nature. As we meditate on God's Word and then obey it, we begin to see His ways and His thoughts, and this in turn leads to success. Unfortunately, many people have it all backwards. Instead of starting at the beginning (meditation), they start at the end (success) and try to work their way backwards. To have real success, there are no shortcuts.

Take a good look at your life and ask yourself whose definition of success you are pursuing. Does your definition of success align with the Bible's? If so, are you meditating daily on God's Word?

1. If the Bible's definition of success includes me fulfilling my purpose, what exactly is my purpose?
   ____
   ____
   ____

2. Am I fulfilling it? __________________________
   ____
   ____

5.)

LUNCH WITH THE WISEST MAN

Wisdom is supreme; therefore get wisdom.
Though it cost all you have,
get understanding.
Proverbs 4:7, NIV 1984

Recently I was flipping through the channels and came across a country music commercial where a chance to win dinner with your favorite country western music star was being advertised. This type of promotion seems to be quite popular these days, whether it is having lunch with your favorite musician, actor, or athlete.

Imagine winning such a contest with the wisest man on earth. How would you spend an hour or so with such a person? What questions would you ask? Would you use the shotgun approach for a Q & A session, or would you let your guest do most of the talking? What if you were allowed only one question? What would that question be?

Well, we are going to sit down with the wisest man who has ever lived, King Solomon. The Bible says that there will never be anyone equal to King Solomon in wisdom. We will see what he says is the most important thing: what is the principal thing, what is supreme.

In our society, people place a great deal of value on money, social status, material possessions, position, fame, and outward appearances. But we will learn from King Solomon that those external goodies are meaningless. What then are we told by this sage is the most important thing? One word: wisdom.

Take a look at what Proverbs 4:7 in the King James Version has to say:

Wisdom is the principal thing; therefore get wisdom: and with all thy getting get understanding.

I love it! He doesn't go into great discourse. He doesn't need to speak over our heads as many of the intellectuals of our age do. But rather he gives us a simple and straightforward instruction.

Now take a look at what our society prizes most. Is it wisdom? Do you see magazines with the title *The 50 Wisest Men* or magazines featuring articles titled "How to Get a Wise Heart"? Some of our celebrities do the most stupid things regarding drugs, sex, alcohol, and illegal activity, yet these same people are esteemed by many as having it all. However, according to the world's wisest man, many lack the most important thing.

How does one get wisdom? Well, first of all, a distinction between worldly wisdom and godly wisdom must be made. First Corinthians 1 and 2 contrast the two. Here's a look. First Corinthians 1:20 says:

Where is the wise? Where is the scribe? Where is the disputer of this world?

> ***Hath not God made foolish the wisdom of this world?*** (KJV)

James 3:15–17 talks of a wisdom, not from above, but a wisdom that is "earthly, sensual, devilish" (v. 15, KJV). In verse 17, James then describes the wisdom from above in this way:

> ***. . . is first pure, then peaceable, gentle, and easy to be intreated, full of mercy and good fruits, without partiality, and without hypocrisy.*** (KJV)

A line is clearly drawn between the wisdom of this world, which the Bible describes as foolishness, and the wisdom of God, which is the kind of wisdom we are to pursue. How do we attain wisdom from God?

Proverbs 1:7 teaches:

> ***The fear of the Lord is the beginning of knowledge: but fools despise wisdom and instruction.***

Without the fear of the Lord, godly wisdom is not even a possibility. With the fear of the Lord, we have taken STEP 1.

STEP 2 is to ask and believe. James 1:5–6 says:

> ***If any of you lacks wisdom, he should ask God, who gives generously to all without finding fault, and it will be given to him. But when he asks, he must believe and not***

doubt, because he who doubts is like a wave of the sea, blown and tossed by the wind.

Without much understanding of God's Word, it might appear from this scripture that God just drops all this wisdom into our laps, and there are no requirements on the part of the recipient. But there is a part for us to play beyond asking and then believing we receive (faith). And that part is to meditate on God's Word. This is how we access the wisdom that God has made available to us. It's as if God gives us a package labeled "wisdom," but this package has a lock on it. The key that will open this package is meditating on God's Word.

Romans 12:2 says:

Do not conform to the pattern of this world, but be transformed by the renewing of your mind. Then you will be able to test and approve what God's will is—his good, pleasing and perfect will.

By meditating on God's Word, we renew our minds, and as we renew our minds, we begin to know what God's will is.

I believe that Joshua 1:8, a verse I like to use often, says it all. (Notice how meditation and obedience come before wisdom.)

This Book of the Law shall not depart out of your mouth, but you shall meditate on it day and night, that you may observe and do according to all that is written in it. For then you shall make your way prosperous,

and then you shall deal wisely and have good success. (AMP)

God desires for you to walk in wisdom, and He has made it available to you. Are you willing to do your part to receive it?

Let's summarize the steps to receive wisdom.

1. Ask God.
2. Believe that you receive.
3. Meditate on God's Word.

In what areas do you lack wisdom and need to know God's will? List all of them, and then go ahead and take the steps to receive what God has made available to you. ____________________

____

____

6.)

BUDDY SYSTEM

Two people are better off than one, for they can help each other succeed.
Ecclesiastes 4:9, NLT

Who's your buddy? Who helps you stay accountable during the challenging times and gives honest input when you're getting off course? Who lends you a helping hand when your strength is small? Who gives a listening ear when you need to talk, a pat on the back when you need reassurance, and compassion when no one else understands? Who is your cheerleader sincerely wanting you to succeed? This to me is the definition of a buddy. Do you have one?

Having a buddy is not optional, if you want to succeed. That's because God made us for each other. Let's take an expanded look at Ecclesiastes 4:9–10, this time from the New International Version:

Two are better than one, because they have a good return for their labor: If either of them falls down, one can help the other up. But pity anyone who falls and has no one to help them up.

A buddy is so important that this scripture actually says that the person without one is to be pitied. So what if that is you? What do you do? First of all, remember, if Christ lives in you, He promises in Hebrews 13:5, ***"Never will I leave you; never will I forsake you."*** Christ is with you *always*.

But then it's time to do your part and find a buddy. Ask God to bring the right person into your life, and be open to whom He may choose. It might not be exactly the type of person you would originally expect. And finally, if you want to have a friend (buddy), do what the Bible says to do: be friendly! In other words, do all the things that a good friend would do. Proverbs 18:24 says:

> ***A man that hath friends must shew himself friendly: and there is a friend that sticketh closer than a brother.*** (KJV)

Find your buddy and then do all you can to maintain that relationship in a healthy manner. Invest in, nurture, and enjoy your God-given friendship! It will make the journey much sweeter and help you fulfill your calling.

1. Who is your buddy?

   ____

   ____

2. What can you do to be a better buddy

   ____

   ____

7.)

STUD DEFINED

I know, my God, that you test the heart and are pleased with integrity.
1 Chronicles 29:17

If I were to list the biggest studs (as well as the biggest successes) of the Bible and of all time, Daniel would be at the top. This guy had it all. He had good looks and no blemishes; was healthy and strong; came from a royal bloodline; was well favored; was a distinguished leader in his land; was confident, courageous, and bold; and on top of all this, he was extremely wise. In fact, he was ten times smarter than those considered the wisest in the land. He could even interpret dreams.

If Daniel were living in our time, he would look something like this: the second or third most politically influential man in America, handsome, athletic, from an influential family, well respected, a graduate of Harvard, and a Rhodes Scholar. Quite a list, wouldn't you say? From the outside, Daniel appeared to have it all.

However, as good as thosc qualities were, they weren't his best ones. His best qualities came from who he was on the inside. Daniel resolved in his heart to keep himself pure. In Daniel 1:8, we read:

But Daniel purposed in his heart that he would not defile himself with the portion of the king's meat, nor with the wine which he drank: therefore he requested of the prince of the eunuchs that he might not defile himself. (KJV)

This is what set Daniel apart as a truly great man, and we see that God blessed Daniel richly because of his commitment to walk in integrity.

When we contrast Daniel with the types of individuals that our society considers to be heroes, the difference is amazing. They, like Daniel, may have the good looks, strength, ability, confidence, and courage, but for many this is where the similarity ends. When you take a look at the inner lives of many of our "heroes," the picture is a mess. Adultery, failed marriages, pregnant girlfriends (and ex-girlfriends), drug and alcohol issues, and scandals seem more like the norm; but in spite of all this, these individuals are highly esteemed. Their lack of character is either considered a minor flaw or overlooked as totally irrelevant, as we have become a society obsessed with outward appearances.

"What's the big deal?" you may ask. Why does this matter anyway? Unfortunately, we have bought into this model and equate success and value with external achievement. Take a look at youth sports. The way some parents act at their child's athletic activities is embarrassing and disgraceful. Their child starts out oblivious to the ***achievement = value equation***, but it doesn't take long for the youngster to catch on. I'm not picking on youth sports, because you can see this in every facet of activity offered to children, whether it is music, theater, dance, or some other kind of activity. And although these things aren't bad per se, sending the message to children that their value is based on their performance is detrimental to their self-esteem.

So what's the alternative?

How about being a present-day Daniel? Notice that Daniel did achieve much on the outside. But this is not where his value came from, nor is it what marked him as a great man. What made Daniel great was his character, and this character is the thing that promoted him. Take a look at Daniel 6:3:

> ***Then this Daniel was distinguished above the presidents and the satraps because an excellent spirit was in him, and the king thought to set him over the whole realm.*** (AMP)

Where is your emphasis? Are you more concerned about outward appearances, performance, and what others think about you, or is your priority being a person of character and inner excellence?

Examine your character.

1. Do you have an excellent spirit as Daniel did? ______________________________
____
2. What changes do you need to make to be a person of character? ______________________________
____

8.)

PRAY CONTINUALLY

Therefore confess your sins to each other and pray for each other so that you may be healed. The prayer of a righteous man is powerful and effective. Elijah was a man just like us. He prayed earnestly that it would not rain, and it did not rain on the land for three and a half years.
James 5:16-17, NIV 1984

What an awesome promise we have! But would you say most Christians truly believe their prayers are powerful and effective? How much time do you dedicate to prayer daily? This will reveal whether or not you really believe that God answers your prayers.

Maybe your struggle is not whether God answers prayer, but whether He answers your prayer. It is easy for us to believe that God wants to answer someone like Billy Graham, but what about us? Do you think God is interested in answering your prayers?

The story of Elijah is a fascinating one. He was a prophet considered to be a mighty man of God, and he did some extraordinary things. For example, in the eighteenth chapter of 1 Kings, we see him boldly take on the 450 prophets of the idol Baal. He challenged them to a duel of sorts.

This duel consisted not of swords, but of prayer. The 450 prophets would pray to their god, Baal, and Elijah would pray to his God, the true and living God. The one that answered by fire would be considered the true God.

The prophets of Baal set up their altar and prayed all day to their god. They slashed themselves and jumped up on the altar, pleading with their god to ignite the altar, but to no avail. Then it was Elijah's turn. To show the people that his God was the only true God, he had the altar drenched with water. He then confidently prayed to God, and fire fell and consumed the sacrifice.

Elijah made it look like a piece of cake. If he was sweating, you sure couldn't see it. At the end of this chapter, we see Elijah praying for rain after a three-year drought, and God answered his prayer.

As we begin to read the next chapter (chapter 19), we see a completely different Elijah from the chapter before. After Elijah defeated the 450 prophets of Baal, he slew them, which infuriated the queen, Jezebel. She sent Elijah a message that she was going to have him killed. You would think that Elijah would still be on a high from seeing God's miraculous works. God had answered his prayers in igniting the altar in front of the 450 prophets of Baal, and God had also answered his prayer to end a three-year drought. If you look a few chapters previous to this, you will see that his prayers even brought a dead person back to life. Wow, what a prayer life! You would expect this guy to be so full of faith that when Jezebel sent her message of death, Elijah's attitude would have been "Bring it on!"

However, we see a totally different response, one of fear and doubt. Not only was Elijah afraid, but he also ran. And then this prophet, this man of faith, prayed maybe one of his most interesting prayers ever. Take a look at 1 Kings *19:3-4:*

Elijah was afraid and ran for his life. When he came to Beersheba in Judah, he left his servant there, while he himself went a day's journey into the wilderness. He came to a broom bush, sat down under it and prayed that he might die. "I have had enough, LORD," he said. "Take my life; I am no better than my ancestors."

I had to laugh when I read that this prophet said, "I have had enough." What about all his victories? What about his great faith? Here we see the humanity of Elijah. He was tired, worn-out from the fight, and he needed to hear from God. I'm sure he felt alone. He had had enough!

How about you? Do you feel as though you have had enough? Are you ready to throw in the towel? If so, take heart. James 5:16-17 encourages us to keep praying. It lets us know that we are in good company in times of trial. And it urges us to pray earnestly and continually.

Success does not mean we never face trials, discouragement, or disappointments. It does, however, imply that we are focused on our purpose and refuse to quit. So hang on! God's power is available. It's just a prayer away.

1. Do you talk to God daily?

   ____

2. How often?

   ____

3. How long?

   ____

4. Are your prayers answered?

   ____

5. Are you satisfied with your prayer life?

   ____

9.)

WHATEVER YOU ASK FOR

"Have faith in God," Jesus answered. "Truly I tell you, if anyone says to this mountain, 'Go, throw yourself into the sea,' and does not doubt in their heart but believes that what they say will happen, it will be done for them. Therefore I tell you, whatever you ask for in prayer, believe that you have received it, and it will be yours."
Mark 11:22–24

Fulfilling your purpose (the real definition of success) is going to require prayer on your part. In our last chapter, we talked about praying continually. It is just a given that we need help from above. So how do we get our prayer answered?

In the above passage, Jesus tells us that if we speak to a mountain to be thrown into the sea and do not doubt, it will be done for us. We will have *whatever* we ask for in prayer.

I know what you're thinking: "Yeah, right. I can really have whatever I ask for in prayer? I've tried that before, but it didn't work." If that describes you, here are a few things to consider:

1. Was your request in line with God's Word and His will? First John 5:14-15 says,

"This is the confidence we have in approaching God: that if we ask anything according to his will, he hears us. And if we know that he hears us—whatever we ask—we know that we have what we asked of him." If you're not sure whether your request was in line with God's will, your assignment is to find out God's will by studying His Word.

2. Do you have unrepentant sin in your life? Psalm 66:18 says, ***"If I regard iniquity in my heart the Lord will not hear me"*** (AMP).
3. Did you speak your answer? Note the phrase that says "what they *say* will happen." Faith is activated by the spoken word. Remember how you became a Christian, confessing with your *mouth* "Jesus is Lord" and believing in your heart that God raised Him from the dead? What you really believe eventually comes out of your mouth. What's coming out of yours?
4. Did you believe in your heart that you had the answer—even when the situation looked just the contrary? Are you willing to believe God's Word until you see your answer with your eyes?

Take a few moments to think about your prayers. Do you meet these qualifiers?

1. Your prayers are in line with God's Word.

   ____

2. You have a repentant heart. ______________

3. You spoke the answer. __________________

4. You believed that you had the answer.

   ____

10.)

ONLY BELIEVE

While he yet spake, there came from the ruler of the synagogue's house certain which said, Thy daughter is dead: why troublest thou the Master any further? As soon as Jesus heard the word that was spoken, he saith unto the ruler of the synagogue, Be not afraid, only believe.
Mark 5:35–36, KJV

If I were to assign a mantra to my life, it would be the theme of this chapter: only believe.

Think about this for a moment. What would your life look like if you obeyed this commandment 100 percent of the time? How would your relationship with God and your relationships with others look? How would your finances, marriage, child rearing, personal life, and spiritual life be affected? Would your life be characterized by success? No doubt, the answer would be yes.

We are told in Hebrew 11:6 that faith is what pleases God. It's what touches His heart. Imagine, touching the heart of God! Well, that is exactly what happens when you believe that God will do what He has said He would do.

When we look at Jesus' ministry on earth, we see that what moved Jesus was not the needs of the people. What moved Jesus was faith. Are you expecting Jesus to move on your behalf because you have needs? Your needs do not obligate Jesus, but your faith does.

Take a look at Matthew 8:5-10, which tells a story of a man who impressed Jesus with his faith. Look closely at the last verse, verse 10, where we see Jesus marvel at his faith:

When Jesus had entered Capernaum, a centurion came to him, asking for help. "Lord," he said, "my servant lies at home paralyzed, suffering terribly." Jesus said to him, "Shall I come and heal him?" The centurion replied, "Lord, I do not deserve to have you come under my roof. But just say the word, and my servant will be healed. For I myself am a man under authority, with soldiers under me. I tell this one, 'Go,' and he goes; and that one, 'Come,' and he comes. I say to my servant, 'Do this,' and he does it." When Jesus heard this, he was amazed and said to those following him, "Truly I tell you, I have not found anyone in Israel with such great faith."

This centurion was pleading to Jesus on behalf of his servant. As Jesus listened to the centurion, He was impressed with his faith more than with any other person's in Israel. Talk about great faith!

The man's faith resulted in his servant being healed. He is an example of what it means to "only believe." How about you? Would Jesus marvel at your faith?

Whatever you face today, Jesus' call to you is "Do not be afraid. Only believe."

Successfully finishing the course that God has set before you will require that you cast your doubt aside and "only believe."

1. Do you believe that God will do what He has promised? ______________________________

2. Do you believe that God has a good plan for your life? ______________________________

3. Do you believe that with God's help you can and will finish the race? ______________________________

11.)

THE TEETER-TOTTER

But I say, walk and live [habitually] in the [Holy] Spirit [responsive to and controlled and guided by the Spirit]; then you will certainly not gratify the cravings and desires of the flesh (of human nature without God).
Galatians 5:16, AMP

I recently was walking through the Christmas section at a department store and saw a certain Christmas decoration that I pointed out to Scott, my husband, and said, "I want that!" I'm guessing he was a bit surprised because he knows me well enough to know that the decoration wasn't quite my style. It was an electric teeter-totter with Santa on one end and three reindeer on the other end. There, on the very top shelf, Santa and his reindeer were teeter-tottering back and forth. At one moment, Santa would be on top, and in the next moment, it would be the reindeer's turn. I wanted it so badly because occasionally I speak at my church, and as a former teacher, I know that a picture is worth a thousand words. That teeter-totter beautifully illustrated the concept of walking in the Spirit.

When Santa was up, the reindeer were always down, and vice versa. It is the same with walking in the Spirit and walking in the flesh. When one is up, the other must be down. Walking in the Holy Spirit simply means that you are obedient to the instructions in the Word of God, the Bible. And when in your heart you sense the Holy Spirit prompting you to do something or prompting you not to do something, such as saying something, buying something, or going somewhere, you immediately obey. When you submit in obedience to the Holy Spirit, you cannot walk in the flesh. It's just that simple.

Many times we get focused on what we should not be doing. Christians can become so consumed with "Thou shalt not . . ." that they never get around to doing what the Bible tells them to do. You have probably heard someone at one time or another tell you not to think of pink elephants. When you were told that, what thought immediately came to mind? Of course, pink elephants.

If you want to walk in the Spirit in your speech, instead of thinking about all the negative things about others, begin to focus on and start speaking the things you should be saying. If you are endeavoring to live a healthier lifestyle begin to focus on eating healthy and exercising. When you make room for one type of activity, such as obedience, you close the door to the opposite activity, disobedience.

What things in your life are you trying to change by taking the cold-turkey approach? Is it gossiping, smoking, overeating, losing your temper? Instead of white knuckling it through the process, find an opposite activity to replace your negative habit. You can successfully overcome the negative behavior by implementing positive behavior.

Remember the Santa and reindeer teeter-totter. Just as it was impossible for both sides to be up at the same time, so too is it impossible for you to be walking in the Spirit and walking in the flesh at the same time.

List the areas that you struggle with in walking in the flesh. Then for each area, list an opposite activity. An example has been given:

Walking in the Flesh	Walking in the Spirit

Walking in the flesh: Gossiping

Walking in the Spirit: Purposefully giving a sincere compliment about someone you would like to gossip about.

12.)

TOP TEN STUPID MISTAKES

Instead of your [former] shame you shall have a twofold recompense; instead of dishonor and reproach [your people] shall rejoice in their portion. Therefore in their land they shall possess double [what they had forfeited]; everlasting joy shall be theirs.
Isaiah 61:7, AMP

Have you ever made a list of your top ten most stupid mistakes? Now if you suffer from really poor self-esteem, this might not be a good activity to participate in, but if you have average self-esteem or above, I encourage you to do this little exercise for the sole purpose of not taking yourself too seriously. Being able to laugh at yourself is a wonderful gift you can give yourself. It may even lower your blood pressure. And maybe best of all, it will help you enjoy life.

I truly believe that one element of a successful life is a life that has been enjoyed. If you're not sure you agree with this, check out John 10:10 where it says that Jesus came to give us life and life to the full! Now that to me says cnjoyment!

It's a fact of life that we all make mistakes, and some of them are really, really big mistakes. But what can we do about it? We can never wipe them from existence, so what more can we do than learn an invaluable lesson from them? I think we can use our mistakes as a constant reminder that we are human and that *thank God,* we have a Savior, Jesus Christ!

What exactly does a savior do anyway? If you have been hanging around the church or Christians for any amount of time, you no doubt have heard this word used on numerous occasions, but what does *savior* really mean?

The first thing that probably comes to a Christian's mind regarding what our Savior, Jesus Christ, does is that He saves us from eternal destruction. But is that it? Once we surrender our lives to Jesus, we may think that Jesus' role as Savior in our lives is over, but far from it. We daily need the saving grace of our Lord and Savior. Let's take a closer look in Isaiah to get a better idea of some of the areas in which we need our Savior's help.

Isaiah 61 is one of my favorite chapters in the Bible. I especially like the detail that the Amplified Bible gives, so we'll take a look at this chapter from that perspective. When I was a teacher, I loved to use textual bullets. I still do to this day. As we go through select verses from this chapter in Isaiah, I will use them to highlight the main points.

The Spirit of the Lord God is upon me, because the Lord has anointed and qualified me to preach the Gospel of good tidings to the meek, the poor, and afflicted; He has sent me to bind up and heal the brokenhearted, to proclaim liberty to the [physical and spiritual] captives and

the opening of the prison and of the eyes to those who are bound. (v. 1)

- This chapter was written of Christ. He is the one anointed and qualified to preach the gospel of good tidings. The term *anointing* is not a concept we often use in our Western culture, and therefore, we do not understand it. When the Bible was written, anointing someone with oil meant that you were passing on to that person authority, similar to the way we do today in the United States on Inauguration Day. Before this ceremony, the president-elect has no authority or power to rule. However, upon completion of this ceremony, the new president has all the power transferred to him or her. If you have ever watched one of these inaugurations, you have seen the fanfare of the new president being sworn in on the Capitol steps. Shortly thereafter, the president makes the procession to the White House, where he takes up residence for the first time. It really is a dramatic and fascinating ceremony. Likewise, we see in this passage that Jesus is the Anointed One.
- If you're suffering from a broken heart, Jesus has come to bind it up and heal it. Psalm 34:18 says: ***"The Lord is close to those who are of a broken heart and saves such as are crushed with sorrow for sin and are humbly and thoroughly penitent"*** (AMP).
- In what areas of your life are you not experiencing freedom? Your Savior has come to

open your prison door. In what areas are you experiencing spiritual blindness? Your Savior has come to open your spiritual eyes.

- Once you are "in Christ," not only do you become the recipient of these promises, but because what is true of Christ is true of you, you become a distributor of these promises. *You* are anointed to bind up and heal the brokenhearted. *You* are anointed to proclaim liberty to the captives and to open the prison and the eyes of those who are bound.

To proclaim the acceptable year of the Lord [the year of His favor] and the day of vengeance of our God, to comfort all who mourn. (v. 2)

- Jesus has come to bring you His favor. Psalm 5:12, in the Amplified, says, ***"As with a shield You will surround him with goodwill (pleasure and favor)."***
- Is your heart filled with sadness and sorrow? You have a comforter in the promised Holy Spirit.

To grant [consolation and joy] to those who mourn in Zion—to give them an ornament (a garland or diadem) of beauty instead of ashes, the oil of joy instead of mourning, the garment [expressive] of praise instead of a heavy, burdened, and failing spirit—that they may be called oaks of righteousness [lofty, strong, and magnificent, distinguished for uprightness, justice, and right

standing with God], the planting of the Lord, that He may be glorified. (v. 3)

Notice the great exchanges that occur in this verse:

- Consolation and joy *IN EXCHANGE FOR* mourning
- Beauty IN EXCHANGE FOR ashes—Ashes represent those things in your life that have been destroyed, stolen, or damaged.
- The garment of praise IN EXCHANGE FOR a heavy, burdened, failing spirit—Notice that praise is described as a garment. It gives us the picture of something that is put on like a piece of clothing. This is what praise is: something you consciously put on. You put on praise by worshiping God. As you do, your spirit is lifted, and the cares that once seemed insurmountable and overwhelming dissipate.
- Jesus' restoration includes you being called an oak of righteousness. Do you see yourself as lofty, strong, and magnificent, not for your glory but for His?

And they shall rebuild the ancient ruins; they shall raise up the former desolations and renew the ruined cities, the devastations of many generations. (v. 4)

- The ancient ruins are symbolic of the ruins in your life. They are the things that have brought you shame and devastation. What things in your life have been broken down and need to be fixed?

Instead of your [former] shame you shall have a twofold recompense; instead of dishonor and reproach [your people] shall rejoice in their portion. Therefore in their land they shall possess double [what they had forfeited]; everlasting joy shall be theirs. (v. 7)

- This is what is so awesome about our Savior. Not only does He come and make right those things that are wrong, but He takes it a step further and restores times two those things that have been stolen from us. He gives us, according to this verse, double what was forfeited. All those things in our lives that have been robbed, whether because of others or because of our own ignorance, disobedience, or stupidity, Christ has promised to give back and then some.
- Along with experiencing restoration of what has been stolen, we are given everlasting joy. Notice that we are not left with regret, but joy!

Christ completely decks us out! The first piece of clothing mentioned is the garments of salvation. The plural word *garments* indicates that we need more than just the garment of having our soul saved from eternal destruction. Rather, we have need of salvation on many different levels. It may be in relationships; in finances; or in our physical bodies, minds, or spirits. Where do you need salvation?

- We are given a robe of righteousness. We don't have to carry our failures, shortcomings, and regrets around with us anymore.

Regardless of where you are today, what you have gone through, what condition your life is in, or what you have done, you have a promise that your Savior, Jesus Christ, has come to bring restoration. Don't delay. Today is the day of salvation.

List the mistakes you've made that seem to plague you—the mistakes where you need restoration. (These may be your top ten stupid mistakes.)

____

____

____

______________________________Then read Isaiah 61 and see God's plan for your restoration.

Steps to Restoration:

1. Understand what provisions are available to you. These are found in the Bible and include such things as forgiveness, a clean slate, courage, hope, peace, love, and patience.
2. Receive, by faith, the promise of God. You do this by believing that what God's Word says is true.
3. Grow in your faith by finding other scriptures that support the promise of God. For example, if you believe what God says about freedom as Isaiah 61:1 promises, go to the concordance at the back of a Bible (or go to an online Bible source such as www.biblegateway.com) and find all the scriptures that deal with this subject. It will help your faith to grow and will encourage you in the process.
4. Believe that Jesus did come to bring you life that is full! He wants you to enjoy life! (See John 10:10.)

13.)

DOES GOD WANT YOU TO SUCCEED?

"For I know the plans I have for you," declares the Lord, "plans to prosper you and not to harm you, plans to give you hope and a future. Then you will call upon me and come and pray to me, and I will listen to you. You will seek me and find me when you seek me with all your heart."
Jeremiah 29:11–13

Did you know that God created you to succeed? Many people think just the opposite. In fact, their prayers sound like they are trying to convince God to bless them, as if success is their idea and not God's.

People fail for many reasons, but not because it is God's will. God has an assignment for each of us to complete. Completing God's assignment according to His specifications always brings success and victory. Unfortunately, many people create their own assignment. Because their self-appointed assignment seems noble to them, they think God is obligated to bless them.

Imagine a teacher giving her students an assignment. The next day when the assignment is collected, the teacher notices in her stack of papers that one student has completed the wrong assignment. The teacher approaches the student and tells them they have done the wrong assignment and will need to do the one that was assigned. The student then tells the teacher, "I really didn't want to do your assignment, so I did a different one." Is the teacher going to say, "No problem. Feel free to do whatever assignment you wish"? I don't think so.

But this is exactly how some people approach God. They find an activity, idea, ministry, or relationship they want to participate in and then ask God to bless it. Instead of getting under God's faucet and being flooded by God's blessing, they expect God to bring His hose over to them and turn it on. They are then disappointed and maybe even disillusioned when He doesn't act.

Remember this: God is not obligated to bless your project, regardless of how noble and righteous it may appear. The only thing that God is obligated to is His Word. His Word is His bond, and He watches over it to perform it. In Jeremiah 1:12, God says He is ***"watching to see that my word is fulfilled."***

Your number one assignment is obedience to God's Word. As you begin to obey God in all aspects of your life, you will see God open doors to you, doors that lead to His blessing, His provision, and His success.

What projects, activities, or assignments are you pursuing? List them and then ask whether these are God's ideas or yours.

Projects: God's Plan or Mine?

____

____

____

____

____

____

14.)

GET A VISION

Where there is no vision [no redemptive revelation of God], the people perish; but he who keeps the law [of God, which includes that of man]—blessed (happy, fortunate, and enviable) is he.
Proverbs 29:18, AMP

What is the driving force in your life? Do you have something on the horizon that you are pursuing that is bigger than you? I am not a psychologist or a psychiatrist, but my guess is that one common denominator of depressed people is a lack of vision, and conversely, one common denominator of successful people is a clear vision.

God created humans to make progress and to set goals and accomplish them. It is in the DNA of every human being. When we are not true to our God- given call, we are miserable, unfulfilled, and unproductive. However, there is a great sense of satisfaction that we get when we make strides forward. This great sense of satisfaction can come in the most seemingly insignificant jobs. Take, for example, mowing your lawn, cleaning your house, or cleaning out your garage. Completing the task in a satisfactory manner gives you a feeling of accomplishment.

How much more can we get satisfaction from completing a task or accomplishing a goal that has even greater importance than household and lawn chores! Maybe your work feeds people, makes their lives easier in some way, heals their sicknesses, or helps people in a number of other noble ways. When you step outside of yourself and get your eyes off "me, myself, and I," your vision becomes enlarged. You are empowered, and your life takes on meaning. And isn't that something we all want to have? In the oracles of history, we all want our lives to have meaning. It's the cry of every heart to ask and know, "What did God create me for?"

When you follow God's plan, the works you do are eternal. Big or small, prestigious or unknown, when you do it as unto the Lord, you have your reward in heaven. Are you a mom and spend your time loving on your kids by wiping snotty noses, satisfying the fantasy of your three-year-old by pretending with her you're being chased by sharks, or cleaning up her spilled milk? Are you an engineer trying to craft a new design to reduce the production time of a product? It really doesn't matter what type of work you do. When you have a vision, you are empowered.

You may be asking, "But what if what I am doing is not my vision?" My answer would be first, to get a clear vision, and then, to start taking small steps to achieve that dream. If you are a schoolteacher but dream of having your own business building houses, don't quit your job and open shop, hoping that business will start pouring in. Start small. Maybe that means learning the trade from another person and working for that person evenings and weekends. Slowly build your business where it can sustain itself and you. Then you can make the smooth transition from schoolteacher to home builder.

Maybe you are thinking, "What if I don't have a vision at all?" The answer to that question is to find someone who does have a vision and plug into their dream. Vision is contagious. When you are around someone who is full of vision, it rubs off and you can't help but be affected by it. Find someone who has a ministry feeding the hungry. Volunteer at a center that works with kids or the elderly. Get involved in a ministry at church. Just make sure that the director or leader is passionate about what he or she is doing. As you invest in another's passion, you will begin to find yours.

What's your vision? Are you pursuing it?

1. What is the thing that God has placed in your heart that won't let go of you, the thing that stirs your passion? ____
____
____

2. Are you taking steps toward it, even if the steps are tiny? ____
____

15.)

WRITE DOWN THE DREAM

Write the vision and engrave it so plainly upon tablets that everyone who passes may [be able to] read [it easily and quickly] as he hastens by. For the vision is yet for an appointed time and it hastens to the end [fulfillment]; it will not deceive or disappoint. Though it tarry, wait [earnestly] for it, because it will surely come; it will not be behindhand on its appointed day.
Habakkuk 2:2-3, AMP

If I were to ask you about your vision (aka dreams) could you produce a written copy outlining your goals to achieve them? Research shows that the likelihood of achieving a goal that is written down is much greater than achieving the goal that is just a hazy idea in your head. Maybe the dream in your head is not hazy, but rather a vibrant and alive dream that is clear and concise. Still, something happens when you put it down on paper.

I remember sitting in a chapel service when I was a student at Oral Roberts University and listening to the speaker Dr. Eugene Swearingen. At the time, Dr. Swearingen was the CEO and chairman of the Bank of Oklahoma and a professor of graduate business at ORU. Rumor among the ORU students was that Dr. Swearingen was a self-made millionaire and taught at ORU for a salary of one dollar a year. Later on, his interest in education led him to become the president of the University of Tulsa.

At this particular chapel service, Dr. Swearingen talked about dreams and goals. In part of his talk, he strongly emphasized the need to carry your dreams around, written on paper. He reached into his coat jacket and pulled out his dreams and goals. They were written on three-by-five index cards. I don't know why, probably because he was the epitome of success, but whatever the reason, that really made an impression on me, and I have been jotting down my dreams ever since.

So how about you? What are your dreams? Get out a scratch pad and let your imagination run wild. You never know what dream lies dormant just waiting for you to dig it up.

1. If you could have whatever your heart desired, what would your wish list look like? ________________

____

____

____

2. On a piece of paper, jot down every dream you have regardless of how audacious it may seem. Then start praying about those dreams and see which ones God wants you to pursue. ________________

____

____

____

16.)

STRATEGIC PLANNING

It's better to be wise than strong; intelligence outranks muscle any day. Strategic planning is the key to warfare; to win, you need a lot of good counsel.
Proverbs 24:5-6, MSG

All successful people have a dream of what they want to accomplish. Once you have a dream, then comes the task of setting goals to achieve that dream. You may have heard of a SMART goal. SMART is an acronym for the following:

- S = Specific
- M = Measureable
- A = Achievable
- R = Relevant
- T = Timeline

I like the SMART acronym, but I have also added some elements to it that I believe are important as well. Here are some guidelines for you to use in strategically planning your goals.

- **SPECIFIC**—Don't be vague. What does it look like, feel like, smell like, taste like, sound like? Be as specific as possible.

- **PASSION**—Is it your passion, or are you doing it merely to impress or please someone else?
- **TIME LINE**—When are you going to arrive at your dream? Give a date and time. If your goal is to get your degree, set up accomplishments along the way. Don't just include your graduation date in two or three years. Where will you be in three months, six months, and one year?
- **TRACKING SYSTEM**—How are you going to track your goal? Is there some way for you to measure it, such as a journal, check-off list, or spreadsheet?
- **REALISTIC**—Is it realistic? With a lot of hard work on your part and tons of grit and determination, is it even possible?
- **BITE-SIZED PIECES**—Plot out small, achievable steps. This will help give you immediate success, which is crucial in keeping the momentum going.
- **MAKE FAILURE IMPOSSIBLE**—Set yourself up for success. Take some time up front to give consideration to all the factors needed for you to succeed. What type of environment is necessary? For example, if your goal is to lose weight, you need to have an environment conducive to this goal. Clear out all tempting and unhealthy foods and drinks. Eliminate as many temptations as possible. What will help you succeed? If your goal is to run a marathon and you are a mom, instead of trying to work it around your husband's schedule, maybe you just need to plan on hiring a babysitter.

- **BACKUP PLAN**—There is one thing I can guarantee: your good intentions will not always go as planned. If you are an all-or-nothing person, you might be tempted to throw in the towel and give up in situations like this. If you have created a backup plan for a brief slipup, a change of plans beyond your control, or a difficulty that you had not seen coming, you will be more likely to continue the course even after you face set-backs. Please, please, please include this in your goals because you will—I repeat, you will—encounter bumps in the road! You can slow down for a bit and even make adjust-ments when they come; just don't let them get you in the ditch.
- **BEST- AND ACCEPTABLE-CASE SCEN-ARIOS**—When going after a goal, I always like to have my ideal scenario (what is pos-sible if everything goes my way) and then an acceptable scenario (what I would be happy with in case things don't go exactly my way). For example, if you are planning on becoming debt free, you might have a pie-in-the sky scenario that would require extreme financial discipline and sacrifice, but you could also have an acceptable scenario that would obvi-ously take longer but not be quite as difficult a goal to achieve. If you want to lose weight before a certain date, giving yourself a range (a best-case scenario of thirty pounds and an acceptable-case scenario of twenty pounds) will give you some breathing room and a real-istic goal to shoot for.

With your goals firmly in place, you will be ready to pursue your dreams. I have included a table below for you to record your dreams. Do they meet the above criteria?

Dream	Specific	Passion	Time Line	Tracking System	Realistic	Bite-Sized Pieces	Make Failure Impossible	Backup Plan	Best- and Acceptable-Case Scenarios
1.									
2.									
3.									
4.									

17.)

AS A MAN THINKETH IN HIS HEART, SO IS HE

For as he thinketh in his heart, so is he.
Proverbs 23:7, KJV

When we talk about goal setting, we frequently refer to the "carrot," that little incentive placed just inches in front of the horse to motivate him to make forward progress. The only problem with this scenario is that no matter how many steps the horse takes, he still is no closer to actually getting to the carrot.

Sometimes going after our dreams can be a lot like the horse going after the carrot. Have you ever made a goal to be more loving, more disciplined, or more positive? You set out on your ambitious goal and hope to arrive at your destination in a few weeks or months.

I remember setting the goal to be more disciplined. Because I knew enough about goals and how to achieve them, I set an end date a few months down the road. Unfortunately, a few weeks later, I realized that I was not even close to achieving my goal. And by the end date of my goal, I had to concede defeat. I literally replayed this scene time and time again.

My problem: I did not see myself as a disciplined person. Instead, I viewed myself as hoping to one day arrive at my destination, also known as *discipline.* It wasn't until I realized that in order for me to be a disciplined person, I had to do the things that a disciplined person did, starting *today.* Not only did I have to *do* those things today, I had to *see* myself as a disciplined person. This attitude caused me to start asking myself how a disciplined person would act in certain situations and then to do it.

Each day I set out with the attitude that I was disciplined and therefore had no other choice but to do what a disciplined person would do. The way I saw myself dictated my actions. It didn't take long, and I really didn't have to give much thought to what I needed to do. I just did it. I was acting out the part of a disciplined person.

The same applies to you. How do you see yourself? Do you see yourself as a loser, a failure, not worthy of love? If so, this is exactly how you will act. The good news is that in Jesus Christ none of these statements are true of you. To the believer, the Bible is full of the promises of God. It resounds with our being persons of significance and extreme value.

Begin to see yourself—and then act—as the Bible says you are. As you do, your behavior will begin to go through a radical transformation.

There's a quote that says something along the lines of "act now like the person you want to become." What practical things can you do today to act like the person you want to become?

1. ____
____

2. ____
____

3. ____
____

4. ____
____

18.)

DON'T BE DECEIVED

Do not be deceived: God cannot be mocked. A man reaps what he sows.
Galatians 6:7

Take an inventory of your life. What do you find? If your life could be compared to a fruit garden, would it abound with succulent and delicious fruit, or would it resemble an overgrown garden full of weeds?

Look at the following areas and make a mental note of the fruit that has been produced in your life:

- Social—How are your relationships with your family, your friends, your coworkers, and your community? Is there peace or friction, good will or jealousy, forgiveness or bitterness, love or hatred, kind words or words of strife, kindness or malice?
- Physical—How is your body faring these days? Are you disciplining yourself with exercise, healthy eating, and healthy lifestyle choices, or are you a victim of compulsive and uncontrolled urges? Do you smoke, drink in excess, do drugs, have unhealthy eating habits, or stress your body by overworking?

- Financial—How does your financial situation look? Have you bought into the lie that material possessions equal success? Do you spend more than you make? Are you undisciplined in your spending? Do you invest for the future? Do you stretch yourself month after month? Are you greedy and consumed with having more money? Do you spend all your money on yourself, or are you tithing and richly blessing others with your money? Are you just plain stressed out about your finances?
- Mental—How is your thought life? Do you spend your time daydreaming and fantasizing? Do you spend your time thinking impure thoughts? Are you plagued with worry, regret, or fear? Do you have peace of mind, or do you find that you can never be by yourself because of your tormenting thoughts? Are you consumed with addictive or destructive behavior? Is your primary focus centered on *you*?
- Spiritual—How is your relationship with God? Do you spend time with Him every day, learning His ways and His thoughts by reading His Word? Are you obeying His Word? Do you spend time in prayer? Are you plugged into a church that you not only receive from but also contribute to? Does God come first in your life, or does He get the leftovers, if there are any?
- Professional—Do you honor God with your vocation, whether that is as a banker, a plumber, a teacher, or a stay-at-home mom? Are you honest in your dealings? Do you treat your employer or employees with

respect? Do you lie about the time you actually work? Do you spend company time doing personal errands? Do you cheat on your taxes?

- Personal—Are you honest, loyal, faithful, and disciplined? Is the time you spend on personal endeavors pleasing to God? Do you spend an abundance of time doing unproductive things such as watching television, being on the computer, or other self-indulgent activities? (Before you throw this book out, let me clarify. I'm not against watching television or being on the computer unless it is excessive, is done at the expense of something more important, or involves inappropriate programming or activities that are in violation of God's Word.)

After a quick checkup, how did you fare? What kind of fruit is your life producing? Are you happy with the harvest, or would you prefer a different scenario? Does your life match the picture of success as seen in the Bible, or is your life a train wreck?

God is very clear in Galatians 6:7 that what we sow is what we reap. When we sow seeds of discord, envy, and jealousy, we are guaranteed to reap broken relationships. When we sow infidelity in our marriage, we are promised to reap heartache down the road.

The key here is, down the road. And this is where we get duped. The fruit never appears immediately after the seed is sown. There is always a span of time between the cause and effect, the choice and the consequence. That is precisely why God tells us in the beginning of Galatians 6:7 not to be deceived.

Take the married man who has a fling with his secretary. If his family unit was immediately torn apart, he was financially burdened by having to provide for two households, and his relationship with his kids was strained or destroyed, he might not be so quick to flirt with the secretary.

Do you think that Bernie Madoff, the investor who cheated numerous people out of billions of dollars, would have chosen to continue his Ponzi scheme if he had known that the next day he would be facing jail time, along with the utter contempt of society? Would Tiger Woods have started his string of trysts had someone flashed before him the price he would have to pay when his secret was uncovered? The obvious answer is no. Both Bernie and Tiger were deceived into thinking that their choices had no consequences.

These are public examples of wrong choices, but we have all been there to some degree. Our lives may not be under the microscope of the public eye, but we all, sooner or later, will reap a harvest from the seeds that we have sown. Some people may shudder when they think of the harvest that they have coming. For others, the harvest can't come soon enough. What will your harvest look like?

Many times when people reap bad consequences they don't, can't, or won't connect the dots. Who then gets the blame? Often it's God. Proverbs 19:3 says:

> ***A man's own folly ruins his life, yet his heart rages against the Lord.*** (NIV 1984)

Are you blaming God for something that is due to the choices you have made? The situations in your life may be the result of the consequences of previous choices. And those choices may have been made years before.

I once read an author's take on how he handled people's mistreatment of him. He said that when someone would do something wrong or hurtful to him, he would ask God, "Are they sowing, or am I reaping?" Great question.

Before I conclude this chapter, I have two words of encouragement. First, if your life looks like a garden overgrown with weeds from a lifetime of bad choices, the good news is that you can choose *today* to change your course. You can begin *today* to sow good seeds. It may take time for those seeds to come up and produce the kind of harvest you desire, but remember the verse we have been focusing on: "Do not be deceived. . . . A man reaps what he sows." Eventually, if you continue to sow good seeds, you will reap a good harvest.

What about the bad seeds that you have sown? They will produce a harvest, but God will give you the grace to deal with those consequences and move on. It may be that you can soften the blow, so to speak, and make restitution. The Bible tells us in Proverbs 28:13:

Whoever conceals their sins does not prosper, but the one who confesses and renounces them finds mercy.

The punishment is usually not as severe when we have the character to confess. As 1 Corinthians 11:31 says:

> ***But if we judged ourselves, we would not come under judgment.*** (NIV 1984)

That's not to say that you won't have consequences to pay, but at the very least, you will be taking a step towards being a person of character and can put that nagging conscience to rest!

Just start planting good seeds *today*! The sooner you plant, the sooner you will reap a harvest.

The second word of encouragement is for those who have been making the right choices, but it doesn't seem to be paying off. Again, remember Galatians 6:7: *"Do not be deceived. . . . A man reaps what he sows."* God does have a payday. It may not be according to your timetable, but He will settle all accounts; and when He does reward you, it will be incredible! So hang in there—your payday is coming!

You don't have to be the victim of your choices. You can choose today to have the kind of successful life that you desire by sowing the right kinds of seeds.

Examine your life.

1. Is it bearing good fruit?________________________
   ____

2. What choices have led you to where you are today? ____________________________________
   ____

3. Have you been making good choices or bad choices?
   ____
   ____

4. What changes, if any, do you need to make *today*?
   ____
   ____

19.)

THE GARMIN LESSON

And we know that in all things God works for the good of those who love him, who have been called according to his purpose.
Romans 8:28

Have you ever been given an illustration and immediately the lightbulb came on? It's as though you get a revelation or an answer that is all of a sudden crystal clear.

That's what happened to me one morning in church as I listened to one of my pastors speak about how God directs our steps after we have taken a wrong turn. He related it to the Garmin Global Positioning System (GPS). It's actually pretty cool how the more sophisticated models talk to you, telling you when to turn, the names of streets, and other valuable information. When you make a wrong turn, it doesn't tell you to turn around and go back so that you can make the correct turn; rather, it redirects you so that you ultimately make it to your destination. The route may not be the original one, but the destination is the same.

What an excellent analogy! I don't know about you, but I have made quite a few wrong turns in my life. When this occurs, it's easy for us to think that our situation is hopeless and unredeemable.

It may feel as though we'll never arrive at where we are supposed to, but when we get hooked up with God, He sees to it that we make it to our final destination. That is, of course, as long as we cooperate with His plan.

The Bible is a great source of inspiration, chock-full of Bible heroes who blew it but ultimately came out victorious. If you are feeling bad about your performance, encourage yourself with the stories of these Bible characters who made big blunders yet were used by God in incredible ways:

<u>Peter</u>—The man that Jesus said He would build His church on betrayed Christ not once, but three times.

<u>Paul</u>—The man who wrote more than two-thirds of the New Testament started out killing Christians.

<u>Abraham</u>—The man whom the Bible calls the "father of faith" got impatient (and in doubt; aka, out of faith) and tried to bring God's promise to fulfillment by his own strength.

Amazingly, we consider all these flawed humans to have been great successes!

Where have you missed a turn? Maybe it was accidental, or maybe it was deliberate. Regardless, if you are beating yourself up over it, God's got a better way for you to live—free from condemnation (see Romans 8:1).

If you have taken a wrong turn and can't seem to get over it, remember God's Global Positioning System (GPS). God will redirect you and get you back on track. Your part in the process is to acknowledge your wrong turn or failure; repent and make restitution, if necessary; and then trust God to fulfill His Word to work *all* things (yes, even your mess-ups) for your good. There may be some extra turns you have to take, and you may have to go out of the way a bit before you make it to your destination, but you will get there if you hang in there with God. So don't be discouraged; just follow the prompts.

1. Is it time to put your mistakes, misfortunes, and your past to rest once and for all? ______________
____
____

2. Can you trust God's amazing grace to work all things for your good? ______________________
____
____

20.)

LIVE PURPOSEFULLY

Look carefully then how you walk! Live purposefully and worthily and accurately, not as the unwise and witless, but as wise (sensible, intelligent people), making the very most of the time [buying up each opportunity], because the days are evil.
Ephesians 5:15–16, AMP

When I think of living purposefully and successfully, I think of my good friend Mr. Babcock, who is lovingly called Uncle X by my three-year-old (my friend's name is Rex, and "Uncle X" was the closest my daughter could get when she first started talking). Most people call him Mr. Babcock because he is sort of like that beloved teacher that you can never bring yourself to call by his first name even twenty years after you have graduated.

Mr. Babcock is an icon in my town of nearly ten thousand people. I first met Mr. Babcock when I moved into the community to be a teacher. He, too, was a high school teacher, and he lived across the street with his wife, Jennifer, and son, Ben. They immediately welcomed me with a visit to my house, bearing gifts of fresh produce from their garden.

We became fast friends, and because I was a single gal, Mr. Babcock and Ben would help me with repairs and yard work. They even gave me a lawn mower. If I ever needed to talk about a situation at school, I could always count on Mr. Babcock to give sound advice.

When it comes to teaching, Mr. Babcock is the consummate teacher. His students love him. His sense of humor and sincere concern for people make him a friend to all. If you were to visit his class before or after school, you would find his classroom packed with students getting help with their trigonometry, calculus, or geometry. As the math department head, he has been instrumental in placing our public high school at the top in our state for state testing scores. He has received many teacher awards, both statewide and nationally.

Not only is Mr. Babcock dedicated to his students in the classroom, he also takes an active role in their extracurricular activities by keeping score at their ball games or taking pictures of them in their many activities. Mr. Babcock takes literally thousands of pictures of students throughout the school year (he told me he takes about six thousand pictures each school year), and at the end of the school year, he gives the majority of the seniors a little photo album full of pictures of themselves participating in their different activities. Pretty impressive considering the senior class ranges between 130 and 160 students.

Mr. Babcock serves his church as a deacon, mows lawns for the elderly, and heads a Relay for Life team that raises thousands of dollars every year for cancer research. He also takes wedding pictures and gives the proceeds to this same organization. Oh, did I mention that he is a Gideon?

When you see Mr. Babcock, you can't help but see a man who lives purposefully, worthily, and accurately. His life is a success. He's fulfilling his purpose—touching one life after another. There is nothing vague or aimless about his life. If your life was under the microscope, would people be able to see the same degree of purpose in your life as Mr. Babcock has in his?

Of course, the ultimate example of living purposefully is Jesus Christ. He knew His mission and purpose and followed it to a tee. Luke 2 gives us a glimpse of Jesus at the tender age of twelve. He and His parents were in Jerusalem for the Passover. Jesus became separated from His parents, and although they desperately searched for Him, they could not find Him for three days. When they finally did locate Him, He was not found playing with other kids or entertaining Himself with some other activity; rather, He was found in the temple having discussions with the scribes. Listen to the answer that Jesus gave His exasperated parents when they questioned Him about where He had been:

How is it that you had to look for Me? Did you not see and know that it is necessary [as a duty] for me to be in My Father's house and [occupied] about My Father's business?
Luke 2:49, AMP

Even Jesus knew His life was not His own. In John 6:38, again in the Amplified, He said:

For I have come down from heaven not to do My own will and purpose but to do the will and purpose of Him Who sent Me.

Mr. Babcock is a great example of what it looks like to live as Jesus did, who served others rather than Himself. Are you living for something bigger than yourself, or is your agenda primarily focused on *you*? Something awesome happens in people's lives when they begin living for a bigger cause than themselves. What's your cause?

What is your cause and your purpose?

____

________________This can also be referred to as your "mission statement."

If you don't have one, take some time to develop one. It will give direction and a whole new meaning to your life.

21.)

PLUG INTO THE POWER SOURCE

I have strength for all things in Christ Who empowers me [I am ready for anything and equal to anything through Him Who infuses inner strength into me; I am self-sufficient in Christ's sufficiency].

Philippians 4:13, AMP

I remember the first time I ever heard this verse. I was a freshman in high school, and some family friends had come over to our house for a visit. One of them was a big basketball fan, and since I played basketball, he grabbed a basketball and went outside with me to shoot a few hoops. As we were shooting, he asked where my favorite shot was and threw me the basketball. I took the shot and totally missed the basket. He rebounded and threw me the ball. Again I took the shot from the same place, and once again I missed. A bit embarrassed, I said, "I can't make it," to which he replied, "I can do all things through Christ who strengthens me." He made me repeat the verse after him and then threw me the basketball again. This time the ball went *swoosh*.

This incident really made an impression on me, and from that time on, I began saying this verse frequently. I am not suggesting you can say this verse and—*poof!*—whatever you say will come to pass. Saying God's Word is not like a magic wand that you wave around and voilà, you have your wish. Being given the promise to do all things does not mean that you can take on any endeavor that you wish and expect God to cause you to succeed. Rather, this verse promises that whatever assignment God gives you to complete, He also gives you the power to do.

What assignment has God given you? Loving your neighbor as yourself? Keeping a bridle on your tongue? Following through on the business idea that God has put in your heart? Setting a goal and accomplishing it?

How can you tap into God's power that He promises to give? You tap into God's power by plugging into God through His Word and through prayer. Every time you have quiet time alone with God, you are tapping into His power. When you listen to the Word being preached, sing praise and worship songs, attend a Bible study, or participate in spiritual activities that focus on God, you are being strengthened and God's power is flowing to you.

If you are in Christ, the Spirit of God lives in you (see chapter 2), but you must plug into the power source. It is equivalent to wanting a piece of toast but refusing to plug the toaster into a receptacle. It doesn't matter how many receptacles you have in your house; you are not going to get toast unless you plug that toaster in. The power is there, but it does you no good until you tap into it. Jesus talked about this very thing in John 15:4:

Remain in me, as I also remain in you. No branch can bear fruit by itself; it must remain in the vine. Neither can you bear fruit unless you remain in me.

Have you tapped into the vine? Are you plugged into the power source? A break in the circuit will cause the power to be cut off. Get plugged in today and see God's power flow to you.

Are you plugged into God via reading His Word and prayer?

__________________________________ Fulfilling your purpose and living a successful life are dependent on the amount of time you spend in the Word and in prayer. If you are feeling frustrated and defeated, ask yourself, "How much time do I spend with God daily in these two endeavors?" __________________________

____

____

Your answer may be revealing. Is it time for you to set aside time daily for reading God's Word and prayer?

____

____

22.)

FORGET THE PAST

Brothers and sisters, I do not consider myself yet to have taken hold of it. But one thing I do: Forgetting what is behind and straining toward what is ahead, I press on toward the goal to win the prize for which God has called me heavenward in Christ Jesus.
Philippians 3:13–14

What an inspiring scripture written by the apostle Paul, who wrote most of the New Testament! He obviously dealt with his past, just as we have to do, yet was determined that he would accomplish what God had called him to do. It might be tempting to think, "That's easy for you to say, Paul. You don't know what I'm dealing with in my past." Surely his past wasn't all that bad, at least not as bad as ours.

Well, let's take a look at what Paul might have struggled with from his past. Before his conversion, Paul was a religious zealot who killed Christians. No doubt he still had images of his victims as they were about to be martyred. Maybe he had flash-backs of the martyrs' families pleading with him to have mercy on their beloved family members. Killing another person, even in the case of self–defense, no doubt leaves a mark on a person. But in Paul's case, it was cold-blooded murder—and not once, but time and time again.

Obviously, Paul knew that if he were to win the prize that God had called him to, he would have to leave the past behind. The same is true for us. To move forward, we must release ourselves from the past. Sometimes forgetting the past means not just leaving our failures behind, but leaving all our successes and victories behind as well. Jesus said it this way in Luke 9:62:

> ***No one who puts a hand to the plow and looks back is fit for service in the kingdom of God.***

If you are struggling with leaving your past behind, let it go! It is what it is, and you can't change it. God has a promise for better things ahead. Here's just a sample:

- Restoration—Isaiah 61 and Joel 2:25–26
- He will work *all* things for good—Romans 8:28.
- His plan is to prosper you and not harm you—Jeremiah 29:11.
- Blessing if you will obey—Deuteronomy 28

Don't let your past hold you back one more day. Leave it behind and take hold of the good life God has for you.

When we reflect on the past and learn from it, it becomes our teacher. When we live in regret over our past, it becomes our tormentor. The beauty is that we get to choose: classroom or prison cell? Which one describes your life? ____
____
____
____

23.)

SMALL BEGINNINGS

Do not despise these small beginnings.
Zechariah 4:10, NLT

Being a runner, I set a goal of running a marathon before I turned forty. I also wanted to have children (hopefully before forty), and since I knew that training for a marathon and having small children would be extremely challenging, I made it my goal to run my first marathon before I ever got pregnant. So in January of 2005, I began my training and shortly thereafter registered for a marathon scheduled for May.

Paying the fifty dollars to register cemented my decision. I knew I was committed. I really didn't know much about training for a marathon, but I enjoyed reading running magazines and was motivated by their articles on training for marathons. I got on a marathon guru's website and printed out his training schedule. I followed his schedule to a tee.

After I had trained five and a half months, the day finally arrived. Scott and I woke early and arrived at the start of the race in plenty of time for me to register, stretch, and prepare for the race. The other runners did the same, and you could sense the excitement and anticipation. At this point, all I wanted to do was start the race!

At the starting line, there was a DJ on an intercom getting the runners pumped up for the race. Butterflies were fluttering in my stomach, and my heart was pounding. I was ready! Finally the race began.

Looking back, I see that the marathon had much more of a dramatic start than most of my projects do. Most of the goals I set out to accomplish don't begin with the fanfare of a race. There's no music, no DJ, and, in most cases, no one else who is running the same race. It's usually a quiet beginning, and more frequently than not, the beginning is small.

It's easy to think that small beginnings are insignificant and unimportant. However, in Zechariah 4:10, we are reminded not to despise the day of small beginnings. In fact, it seems as though that is God's trademark: starting small.

Think of how our Savior, Jesus Christ, came into the world. It had been prophesied many centuries earlier that Jesus would come to the earth to save the world from sin. In Revelation, we see Jesus riding on a white horse and defeating Satan once and for all. You would expect the Savior of the world to come to earth in a spectacular way, maybe riding in a chariot with a procession or appearing in a cloud of glory. But that is not the way Jesus came to earth. He came in the most humble way, as a baby. And that baby was not born in a palace or even in a house, but in a lowly stable. Jesus' beginning on earth was small, but look at the significance of His life.

In working with teens and young people, I commonly see kids and young adults who have mistakenly fallen into the trap of believing "if God is involved, it's got to be big!" Don't get me wrong. I do believe God gives big dreams, but instead of taking one small step after another, many individuals want to have it all on day one.

I've seen people open businesses, and instead of using the resources they have and slowly adding little by little, they furnish the place with the best furniture and the most sophisticated computers, spending a small fortune. Their assumption is that their idea is going to be a big hit, so going into tremendous debt is just the price they have to pay because, after all, they'll be getting their investment back immediately. Inevitably, things don't turn out as planned, and although they start big, they don't end big. In most cases, they don't finish at all.

Want to start a business? Start with what you have. Maybe that means converting a tiny space in your basement into an office. Maybe it means not quitting your job but rather working your business on evenings and Saturdays until you have established something that can sustain itself.

Want to work as a missionary, minister, or song leader? Instead of thinking you have to have a full-time position beginning immediately, start being faithful where you are. Serve in someone else's ministry. Luke 16:12 says:

> ***And if ye have not been faithful in that which is another man's, who shall give you that which is your own?*** (KJV)

Remember the tortoise and the hare. Be content with the small steps immediately in front of you. They are the steps that will be your teachers and help grow your character. And they are the steps that will ultimately lead you to success.

What are the small steps you can begin taking today?

1. ______________________________
____

2. ______________________________
____

3. ______________________________
____

4. ______________________________
____

5. ______________________________
____

24.)

FINISH STRONG

However, I consider my life worth nothing to me; my only aim is to finish the race and complete the task the Lord Jesus has given me—the task of testifying to the good news of God's grace.
Acts 20:24

I love new beginnings. It is always so exciting to start a new project or a new goal. I am actually writing this on December 31. This evening many will be celebrating the New Year. Along with the New Year will come many resolutions and goals. And though we like to think about the New Year with high hopes and expectations, we very rarely think about finishing out strong the previous year. How many times have we made a resolution, say, to lose weight or get on a budget, and then tell ourselves we better splurge the last few days of December because we want to start strong on January 1?

The irony is that although getting a strong start is good, finishing strong is even more crucial to our success. In fact, we see a lot of people who did not get a strong start in life, but who defied the odds and overcame adversity to achieve incredible feats. We don't really talk about and focus on their beginnings, but we do focus on their finishes.

Remember Michael Phelps and his winning of the hundred-meter butterfly at the 2008 Olympics? It looked as though he was going to earn his first silver medal (after winning six previous gold medals), but with his strong finish at the last second, he surprisingly won yet another gold. I guess you could say Michael finished strong, bringing home eight gold medals and shattering Mark Spitz's thirty-year record.

I sometimes wonder if we place too much emphasis on starting rather than on finishing. It really doesn't take much to get started. In most cases, our emotions are so revved up we don't have to put much work into the first steps. Discouragement has not yet hit, as well as the reality of what it is going to take to get the job done. If you have ever played sports, you can probably remember that first day of practice, filled with excitement for the new season. Fast forward to the end of the season when those emotions were long gone and there was nothing exciting about practice. In fact, many of the athletes were already looking forward to starting the next sport or activity.

I can remember the excitement I had the first day of the school year when I was a teacher. I would wake up early (without an alarm clock), jump out of bed, have my quiet time, get a workout in, and be at school an hour before the kids arrived. I was ready to greet my little darlings with a big smile and "Welcome to the new school year!" I did not need to rely on discipline to wake myself up on those mornings. My excitement nearly catapulted me out of bed.

Compare that to my actions in January and February, the longest two months of the school year. It was very cold and dark when I woke up, and I had zero emotions of excitement at five or so in the morning. That is when I had to rely on self-control and discipline. My emotions had gone on vacation.

Finishing strong is a habit. Unfortunately, so is quitting or finishing in a sloppy and careless manner. It is really easy to look at the little things in life and think they are not that important. Sure, we know that it is important for an Olympian to finish his race strong, but finishing that little project at home or fulfilling that commitment at church doesn't seem like that big of a deal.

But it is a big deal, and how you finish one project will determine how you begin the next. So before you are tempted to throw in the towel on your current projects in hope of a fresh, new start, finish strong those things you have already started. In doing so, you will develop not only self-discipline, but also a spirit of excellence.

What grade would you give yourself on finishing what you start?   A   B   C   D   F

Are there any projects that you have left unfinished but that you know God wants you to complete? Fill them in below, and then take the first step towards getting them completed.

1. ______________________________
   ____

2. ______________________________
   ____

3. ______________________________
   ____

4. ______________________________
   ____

25.)

A LITTLE TASTE OF SUCCESS

The way to develop self-confidence is to get a record of successful experiences behind you.

William Jennings Bryan

Being from a small town of about three hundred, I enjoyed a lot of perks. I particularly enjoyed attending its small school. My graduating class had fifteen students in it, and although the number in our school was small, the opportunities were many.

Grades K through 12 were all on the same campus. The junior high and high school were in the original school building that my dad (as well as Hubert H. Humphrey, former vice president of the United States) had attended when he was in high school. Built in the early 1900s, this building was connected to the newer elementary school. The parking lot for students who drove to school was located so that in order to get to the junior high and high school, you had to walk down the long hall of the elementary school. This really gave you a feeling of being connected with the entire school. Throughout your school day, you would frequently get to see kids of all different ages and grade levels. Later on, when I was a teacher in a much larger high school, I really missed the close-knit family atmosphere of a small school.

Sports were a big deal in my school, and although basketball was my love, I, like many of my friends, went out for any sport available, even if it wasn't necessarily my favorite. Track was one of those sports. The first opportunity to be involved in sports came in the seventh grade, and because of our school's small numbers, the junior high athletes practiced with the high school athletes and were placed on the third or fourth string. When it came to track, unless you were really fast (which I was not), you were placed in all the events that were left over after the high school athletes had chosen their events. So as a seventh-grade trackster, I found myself signed up for the mile race, along with my friend Lisa. Being good friends, we made a pact that we would run together. This meant a lot to me because not only was I not very fast, but I also had a bum knee, which caused me to run at an even slower pace. I pretty much just hobbled around the track.

At one particular track meet, Lisa and I were just finishing our second lap as other runners were sprinting past us finishing the race. They had finished their entire four laps before we had finished our first two laps! As we began our third lap, two senior boys from our school came along the track and shouted, "Coach says to get off the track!" Now some might find this experience humiliating, but as seventh-graders, we were thrilled that the race was over!

Fast forward to my junior year of high school. It was fall and girls' basketball season had just begun. This was the sport I absolutely loved. My basketball coach had been named the cross-country Coach of the Year in South Dakota at the previous school where he had coached. Just for the fun of it, he asked if any of us basketballers would be interested in running in a cross-country meet. The meet would get us out of school and cause us to miss basketball practice, but as an incentive for us to run in the meet, he was leaving the assistant basketball coach with a tough practice schedule. So the choice was cross-country meet or tough basketball practice.

The coach got only four takers for the meet, and I was one of them. Although I had been pretty pathetic in junior high, I had begun to run on my own and was really starting to enjoy it. I didn't know how I would do, but the thought of running on a golf course sounded intriguing.

The meet was the conference cross-country meet. Our team consisted of a sophomore, two eighth-graders, and me. Because our school had not competed in a cross-country meet for a few years, we really didn't know what to expect. The race started, and to my pleasant surprise, I ran towards the front of the pack. I absolutely loved it. I couldn't believe I was the same runner as that pitiful runner back in seventh grade.

I finished the race in seventh place. My coach and I were both ecstatic. One of my teammates, an eighth-grader, came in first. The other eighth-grader came in thirteenth, and with our combined places, we were able to take first place as a team, even with an incomplete team. I was hooked.

Running has been a part of my life ever since I ran that first cross-country meet. I love it. But why the difference? I believe it is because I had a little taste of success, and it whet my appetite for more.

In your pursuit of your dream, have you had a little taste of success? If not, how can you set yourself up to win small victories? Forget pie-in-the-sky, all-out success for now. We are talking small successes, because you are much more likely to quit your efforts if you don't experience an occasional victory. You may need to change the parameters of your definition of success. Instead of making a thirty- pound loss your definition of success, why not change it to something more bite-sized, like sticking to an exercise plan, losing three pounds, or eating healthy for a week? You get the picture.

In the Bible, we see the story of David and Goliath, which illustrates this point beautifully. David, a shepherd boy, takes on the giant and wins. It's an exciting story, but this is not David's debut. Let's look at the story in 1 Samuel 17:32–37. We'll begin where David was standing before King Saul, asking for permission to fight the giant:

David said to Saul, "Let no one lose heart on account of this Philistine; your servant will go and fight him."

Saul replied, "You are not able to go out against this Philistine and fight him; you are only a young man, and he has been a warrior from his youth."

But David said to Saul, "Your servant has been keeping his father's sheep. When a lion or a bear came and carried off a sheep from the flock, I went after it, struck it and

rescued the sheep from its mouth. When it turned on me, I seized it by its hair, struck it and killed it. Your servant has killed both the lion and the bear; this uncircumcised Philistine will be like one of them, because he has defied the armies of the living God. The LORD who rescued me from the paw of the lion and the paw of the bear will rescue me from the hand of this Philistine."

Saul said to David, "Go, and the LORD be with you."

David had confidence to slay the giant only because he had small successes under his belt. He had experienced God's strength in the small battles, which in turn gave him confidence in the big battle.

What are the small steps you can begin taking that will lead you to victory? Choose steps that are small and achievable. As you begin to succeed, you can then up the ante a bit. But don't despise the small steps!

Rate your confidence in yourself from 1 to 10 (1 being low and 10 being high). ______________________________

If you suffer from a lack of confidence (anything below a 6 or 7), begin building your confidence by chalking up some small successes. Choose a goal that is just outside your reach but totally achievable. What little success are you going to pursue first?

____

____

____

26.)

FREEDOM LIKE NONE OTHER

Freedom from sin's tyranny is the greatest freedom of all.

Author Unknown

I remember reading the above quote shortly following the war in Kuwait back in 1991. It was around July 4, and many towns in the area where I lived were celebrating Independence Day with parades, concerts, and other festivities. But this year was different. The meaning of freedom was much more poignant than it had been during past Fourth of July celebrations. This year our country not only celebrated the independence that had been won hundreds of years earlier, but it also celebrated the victory the United States had just secured. These celebrations honored the men and women who had made the sacrifice, putting their lives on the line to secure our country's victory. I couldn't help but think of the joy that these soldiers and their families must have been experiencing.

As great as the freedom that we experience in America is, there is an even greater freedom available to us. This freedom is freedom from sin. There is no captor more oppressive and no burden so heavy as sin. Fortunately, there is one who has carried our sin. He is the only one credited with this feat, and His name is Jesus Christ. First Peter 2:24 says:

"He himself bore our sins" in his body on the cross, so that we might die to sins and live for righteousness; "by his wounds you have been healed."

Are you living in bondage to sin? Does your bondage come in the form of an addiction, a habit that you can't break, or thoughts that you are powerless to control? Jesus Christ came to set the captive free. In John 8:36, we are told of the awesome prospect available to those who will receive this free gift of freedom:

So if the Son sets you free, you will be free indeed.

Are you free indeed, or is your life plagued by sin? Success will elude you if you don't settle this issue once and for all. Fortunately, Jesus Christ, the bondage breaker, has already paid the price for your sin. He took care of it at the cross. All you have to do is receive this gift of freedom.

How can you be free in Christ?

1. Christ's freedom is available to all. However, you must be part of the family. If you have not yet taken this step, see chapter 1.
2. Understand that Jesus has already secured your freedom when He went to the cross. All you must do is receive by faith the gift that He has already purchased with His blood.
3. Begin meditating on (thinking and saying) scriptures that talk about your freedom in Christ. Find all the scriptures you can on freedom by looking them up in a Bible's concordance or on a Bible website such as www.biblegateway.com. Write them on index cards, and say them many times a day. The more you meditate on them, the more they will become a part of you. I'll give you a couple to get started:

    - Romans 6:18 says, ***"You have been set free from sin and have become slaves to righteousness."***
    - John 8:31–32 says, ***"If you hold to my teaching, you are really my disciples. Then you will know the truth, and the truth will set you free."***

27.)

WHAT'S IN YOUR HOUSE?

Use the resources you have.

Unknown

When I was a student at a ORU, it was mandatory that students attend chapel twice a week. That didn't matter to me, though, because those chapel services were one of the highlights of my week. I loved them. The praise and worship was awesome, and occasionally there would be a speaker I was really interested in hearing. With all those chapel services under my belt, there are only a few messages I still remember. This one ranks at the top.

The message was given by Tommy Barnett, the pastor of Phoenix First, and its title was "What's in Your House?" He told the story of the prophet Elisha, who encountered a widow pleading with him to help her. Here's the story:

The wife of a man from the company of the prophets cried out to Elisha, "Your servant my husband is dead, and you know that he revered the LORD. But now his creditor is coming to take my two boys as his slaves." Elisha replied to her, "How can I help you? Tell me, what do you have in your house?"

"Your servant has nothing there at all," she said, "except a small jar of olive oil."
2 Kings 4:1–2

This story may be hard for us Westerners to understand. We occasionally see people have their cars repossessed, utilities cut off, or their houses go into foreclosure, but never do we see people required to relinquish their children as payment on a debt. However, under the law of the day (the Mosaic law), servitude was permitted as a way to repay debt. Talk about tough times! Not only was this woman destitute, but she was about to lose her own flesh and blood. But when the prophet heard her predicament, he simply asked, "What's in your house?" to which the woman replied, "Your servant has nothing there at all, except a little oil."

It is our human nature to look outward for the answer to our problems. Especially in our society, we feel entitled to be taken care of. But there is a crucial principle in the wisdom of the prophet's words. He was in essence telling the woman, "The answer is in your house!" The take-home message here is that you will not find your answer in government programs, church programs, lotteries, parents, siblings, and wherever else you think the solution lies.

What things in your life do you lack, and instead of going to work to achieve those things, you make excuses for them? What dream do you have in your heart that you have made excuses for not pursuing? Maybe you think you don't have the time, money, education, socioeconomic background, looks, talent, or resources. Get the picture?

You may have to get creative. But if you want something badly enough, you can have it. Take writing this book. Currently, my daughters are three years old and two years old. I feel called first to my family and feel as though I need to spend time during the day with them, so I spend time writing from 5:00 to 7:00 a.m. It works perfectly. I don't miss time with them in order to spend time on writing, yet I am fulfilling what I believe is also a purpose God has for me.

I'm sure if you take a look around at people in your life, you will see those determined individuals who are working part-time jobs or on the weekends in addition to their full-time jobs in order to pursue a dream or goal.

What is in your house? What talents, gifts, and resources do you have that you could use to make your dreams come true? Maybe it will include providing a service such as trimming trees, giving massages, or building furniture on your days off. Maybe it's time to sell some items or downsize. The point is you have something of value. Maybe you have the passion for something but don't yet have the skill. If so, you may need to take classes or do an apprenticeship. Just do something.

If you are waiting for the floodgates of heaven to open and are not doing a thing, you will be waiting a very long time. Have you ever seen a traffic cop directing parked cars in a parking lot? The obvious answer is no, because traffic cops don't direct parked cars—they direct moving cars.

The same principle applies with God. He does not direct sitting people—He directs moving people.

So pick yourself up, dust yourself off, and begin to take the first steps towards being a success and making your dreams come true.

1. What dreams and desires in your heart have you been putting off? ______________________________

   ____

2. What are the excuses that you have been using to justify not pursuing those dreams? ____________

   ____

3. List every one of these excuses, and then list all the resources that you have "in your house" to fulfill those dreams. ______________________________

   ____

   ______________________________Don't wait another day. Do it today!

28.)

HOW TO GET PROMOTED BY GOD

The LORD rewards everyone for their righteousness and faithfulness.
1 Samuel 26:23

When it comes to being promoted, it's important to understand the premium that God places on faithfulness. It's also important to understand that all promotion does not come from God. How can you tell the difference? Proverbs 10:22 tells us:

The blessing of the LORD brings wealth, and He adds no trouble to it.

When God brings promotion and blessing, there is no trouble attached to it. People can be fooled by a promotion, thinking it must be from God. Take the man who gets moved up the ladder in his company. The only downside is that his new responsibilities take him away from his family most evenings and weekends, ultimately resulting in divorce, unfaithfulness, or strained relationships. This is not God's promotion.

We have already taken a look at Mark 8:36, but it bears repeating:

For what shall it profit a man, if he shall gain the whole world, and lose his own soul? (KJV)

God's promotion will result not only in a blessing financially or personally, but also spiritually. If an opportunity is presented to you, but it will not be conducive to your spiritual growth and well-being, it is not a promotion from God. Wait for God's blessing, because His blessings are *really*, *really* good, and they bring soul peace. This is true success.

We all would like to receive God's promotion. What do we need to do to be on the receiving end?

1.) Be faithful where you are, investing in someone else's dream.

2.) Regardless of the work you are presently doing, do it with all your heart. Make it your ambition to put in more work than you are getting paid for, as well as to be the most valuable employee your boss has. This will make you indispensible and set you up for promotion.

3.) In your current position, act as if you own the company.

By this I don't mean that you boss everyone around and are a know- it-all. Rather, you treat your job, the facilities, and the people you deal with as if the company were your own. This means you don't come in late or leave early. You go the extra mile to make your customers happy. You don't engage in the nit-picking and backbiting that goes on among your coworkers. Instead, you make the place better than when you arrived by fostering a spirit of cooperation and goodwill, as well as demonstrating a desire to be more efficient.

As you begin to add faithfulness to your character, you will begin to see the promotion of God in your life. And it will be promotion like none other you have ever seen!

1. Have you positioned yourself to be promoted by God because of your faithfulness?

____

____

2. What is your level of faithfulness?

____

____

29.)

IT AIN'T ABOUT YOU!

You're blessed when you're at the end of your rope. With less of you there is more of God and his rule.
Matthew 5:3, MSG

Shortly after Scott and I were married, we were invited to a dinner party to get to know some of his colleagues and their spouses. One particular colleague had been a D1 basketball player, and so had his wife. This was the first time I had met her. She definitely left a memorable first impression. She had a commanding personality, was a blond with model good looks, and from what I remember, she was probably about six feet two (not including the four-inch heels she was wearing) and spoke her mind. To be honest, she was quite intimidating, but even so, she was very engaging and fun to talk to.

As Scott and I talked to her, she began to tell us about her three boys and how life changes once you have children. Wagging her finger that seemed as long as a stick and bobbing her head from side to side, she told us in reference to having kids, "It ain't about you." It was such a memorable moment that many times since then, Scott and I have said that phrase while we imitate those mannerisms.

It ain't about you. When's the last time you looked in the mirror and told yourself that? Be honest, because I'm sure there are many people who have never told themselves no. Are you one of them? Especially in this society where instant gratification reigns supreme, denying oneself is not popular.

So if it ain't about you, what is it about anyway? Two words: serving others. Truly successful people understand that life doesn't revolve around them. They see themselves as conduits to help make the world a better place for others. The funny thing is this: as you begin to think of others first and get your mind off yourself, good things start coming your way. It's as if you become a magnet for blessings to be poured out on your life.

Is your sight set outward on others, or are you selfishly focused only on your needs, wants, and desires? Why not, today, become part of something that is bigger than yourself? Offer your services to help someone less fortunate than you. Brighten the day of someone who needs a little encouragement. Get involved with a local charity. Just do something, but get ready.

Research shows that those people who serve others are happier, experience more fulfillment, and have a greater sense of purpose. My guess is that's because they have discovered one of life's little secrets—it ain't about you!

Which statement describes you?

1. It's all about me!

OR

2. It ain't about me!

30.)

HOW TO ACQUIRE TRUE FREEDOM

So Jesus said to those Jews who had believed in Him, If you abide in My word [hold fast to My teachings and live in accordance with them], you are truly My disciples. And you will know the Truth, and the Truth will set you free.
John 8:31-32, AMP

On many occasions, I have heard people, even in the secular world, say, "You will know the truth, and the truth will set you free." For many the truth that they are talking about is truth according to their definition, which is based on their personal beliefs, the beliefs of others, their feelings, or what they think is truth. Maybe they believe that the truth for them is that they no longer love their spouse, so therefore they feel entitled to find a new one. Or maybe they believe that truth for them justifies some other behavior contrary to God's Word.

However, when reading this scripture in its context, we see a totally different picture. There is a qualifier for knowing the truth, and that qualifier is obedience to God's Word. *Then,* we are promised to know the truth, and that truth is what sets us free. But what exactly is this truth?

It is analogous to flying an airplane. When the pilot enters the plane, he places 100 percent of his confidence in the instruments. I have been told that flying, at times, can be totally deceiving to a person's perception of space. You may think you are flying up, but actually the opposite may be true. This is especially the case when flying in cloudy weather or at night. For this reason, the pilot checks his feelings and intuitions at the door. His instruments are the absolute authority.

This is a beautiful picture of truth. Truth, in this case, is the instruments. They are absolute and do not change according to the circumstance. They are constant, reliable, and trustworthy. The pilot has been taught to rely on them completely. Failure to do so could cost him his life.

When it comes to people's lives, many of them live without any instruments. Their truth is whatever they determine it to be. These folks are ruled by what they feel, think, and see or by what others feel, think, and see. They believe there are no absolutes, and rightly so, because if you follow your feelings, there are no absolutes!

Feelings are the most unreliable, fickle, deceiving, fleeting, and manipulating determinants that you can base your decisions on. They are poor indicators of truth, and many times result in bad outcomes. Basing your decisions on the roll of the dice would be just as accurate or maybe even more accurate than going by your feelings.

Now I'm not bashing feelings, because they can be really, really good. And after all, who doesn't like feeling good? But the point I am making is not to base your life and your choices on feelings. Feelings change, but the principles in God's Word do not. That's why humans don't particularly care for them at times. These principles cut into our agendas and challenge our beliefs. At times they are inconvenient and confrontational. Many times they are just downright uncomfortable. And boy, do we like comfort! But this is exactly the point where freedom comes in.

So, to break it down, here are the steps to finding truth and living in freedom:

STEP ONE: Obedience produces understanding and knowledge of the truth. Take a look at how obedience and understanding are related in the following scriptures:

Observe them carefully, for this will show your wisdom and understanding to the nations, who will hear about all these decrees and say, "Surely this great nation is a wise and understanding people."
Deuteronomy 4:6

And unto man he said, Behold, the fear of the LORD, that is wisdom; and to depart from evil is understanding.
Job 28:28, KJV

The fear of the LORD is the beginning of wisdom: a good understanding have all they that do his commandments: his praise endureth for ever.
Psalm 111:10, KJV

The fear of the Lord is the beginning of wisdom: and the knowledge of the holy is understanding.
Proverbs 9:10, KJV

STEP TWO: Understanding and knowledge result in freedom.

You will know the Truth and the Truth will set you free.
John 8:32, AMP

Where are you in the quest for truth? Do you believe there is an absolute truth? Or are you your own compass? Next time you are tempted to find truth outside of God's Word, remember the words of Jesus:

I am the way and the truth and the life. No one comes to the Father except through me.
John 14:6

John 8:36 says, "So if the Son sets you free, you will be free indeed." Ask yourself this question:

"Does this statement describe my life?"

____
____
____

31.)

HOW TO REBUILD A WALL

Let us not become weary in doing good, for at the proper time we will reap a harvest if we do not give up.
Galatians 6:9

Have you ever been faced with a task that seems so daunting that you felt defeated before you even began? It's hard to get motivated when from the get-go things appear insurmountable and success seems unattainable. The book of Nehemiah tells us the story of such a task.

The city of Jerusalem was in ruins. Its walls had been torn down and its gates burned. God gave Nehemiah the assignment of building it up again. Although there were many naysayers, Nehemiah accepted the mission with confidence:

Then I said to them, "You see the trouble we are in: Jerusalem lies in ruins, and its gates have been burned with fire. Come, let us rebuild the wall of Jerusalem, and we will no longer be in disgrace." I also told them about the gracious hand of my God on me and what the king had said to me.

They replied, "Let us start rebuilding." So they began this good work.
Nehemiah 2:17–18

We see from this passage that Nehemiah assessed the situation and believed that God would help bring him success. That was the first step, but that confidence is not what got the work completed. Instead, it was hard work combined with consistency over the long term that was required. For the rest of the next eleven chapters, we read how Nehemiah rebuilt the city little by little. He and his men were faced with many challenges. Not everyone was excited about their rebuilding of the city. They were laughed at, ridiculed, and mocked. In chapter 4, verse 2, Sanballat had the following to say:

What are those feeble Jews doing? Will they restore their wall? Will they offer sacrifices? Will they finish in a day? Can they bring the stones back to life from those heaps of rubble—burned as they are?

Then Tobiah the Ammorite chimed in:

What they are building—even a fox climbing up on it would break down their wall of stones!
Nehemiah 4:3

This chiding did not deter Nehemiah, but rather it strengthened his resolve. In chapter 4, verse 6, Nehemiah explained how the wall was built:

For the people had a heart and mind to work. (AMP)

In chapter 5, verse 16, Nehemiah said:

> ***I also held fast to the work on this wall. . . . And all my servants were gathered there for the work.*** (AMP)

Not only did the people face the task of rebuilding the wall, but they also had to defend themselves in the process. Their enemies did not want them rebuilding the wall, and as a result, they came to fight them. Nehemiah and his men had to build the wall while holding weapons in their hands. But after fifty-two days and with a lot of help, they saw the completion of the task.

Can you relate to Nehemiah? Are there any walls in your life that have been torn down and need repaired? Maybe the process seems overwhelming and you just want to bury your head in the sand. If you will take the approach of Nehemiah and follow his consistency model, you will eventually get your wall repaired. There's a song that goes, "Just put one foot in front of the other." This is good advice. With consistency and determination, you can rebuild the walls in your life one stone at a time.

In what areas of your life do you have broken walls that need to be rebuilt? Regardless of how impossible the task may appear, if God is asking you to build, He will help you successfully finish the task. ______________

____

____

____

32.)

STAY BETWEEN THE LINES

Be well balanced (temperate, sober of mind), be vigilant and cautious at all times; for that enemy of yours, the devil, roams around like a lion roaring [in fierce hunger], seeking someone to seize upon and devour.
1 Peter 5:8, AMP

In our overbooked and hectic schedules, getting out of balance is easy to do. But did you know that in doing so we make ourselves easy prey for the devil's attacks? We may as well paint the bull's-eye on our back and issue the invitation to be devoured. It's not a matter of whether we will be attacked, but when. In essence, when we get out of balance, we are opening a door for the devil to come on in.

It's hard to live the successful life God has called us to when we have opened the door to the devil. When we do that, we find our lives riddled with defeat and failure. So what's the antidote? Being well balanced. In other words, it's leaving some margin in our lives and not overdoing it in any one particular area.

Are you out of balance in some area of your life? Your work? Your hobby? Your recreation? Your spending? Your eating? Your relationships? Don't set yourself up to be destroyed. Stay between the lines.

List the areas in which you are out of balance. How can you stay between the lines in these areas? What changes do you need to make?

1. ______________________________
____

2. ______________________________
____

3. ______________________________
____

4. ______________________________
____

5. ______________________________
____

33.)

FOCUS

Let your eyes look right on [with fixed purpose], and let your gaze be straight before you.
Proverbs 4:25, AMP

Have you ever known someone who is focused? Their whole approach is different from the average person's. They have a purpose and an urgency that seem to direct their course. Contrast that with the person who coasts along with no real drive. They have a lot of time on their hands, which is evident by the way they carry themselves. There is no immediacy about them. They don't accomplish much throughout their day, which doesn't really matter, because to them they have all the time in the world.

When you take a look at the people who have accomplished something of value, they fall into the category of the focused. Think about the Olympic athlete, the med student who becomes a doctor, or the couple who is committed to paying off their credit cards and living debt free. These individuals all have this in common: they are successful because they have focus.

Focus is a powerful force. It concentrates your efforts and eliminates distractions. It may require that you put everything else aside for a time while you give your undivided attention to the task at hand, but it will not disappoint. The final result will be well worth the sacrifice.

One of the greatest examples of all times, when it comes to focus, is Jesus' going to the cross. He had to fix His eyes on the greater good that would result (redeeming mankind) rather than on the pain and sacrifice that would be required of Him. Hebrews 12:2 talks about the focus we ought to have, as well as the focus that Jesus had:

Let us fix our eyes on Jesus, the author and perfecter of our faith, who for the joy set before him endured the cross, scorning its shame, and sat down at the right hand of the throne of God. (NIV 1984)

That's what you call focus. Do you have it? If so, are you focused on the right things?

1. Do you have a focus? ______________________________
   ____

2. If so, is it on the right thing? ____________________
   ____

3. In your heart, what do you believe you are to focus on and give yourself fully to? ____________________
   ____

34.)

LITTLE FOXES

Catch for us the foxes, the little foxes that ruin the vineyards, our vineyards that are in bloom.
Song of Solomon 2:15

Have you ever felt that you were taking one step forward and two steps back? Has success ever seemed far off, and maybe instead of getting closer to the goal, it appears you are only getting farther from it? Sometimes that's just life, but still, it's always good to step back and evaluate.

At times we are shooting ourselves in the foot and don't even realize it. Many times it's the little things that are dragging us down, and we either don't know it or think it doesn't matter.

Maybe it's that bad habit of yours that you think is no big deal or the extra spending each month that adds up over time. Maybe it's an unkind word or a bad attitude that you think is not that big of a deal. But little things are a big deal, and they do add up.

If you want to have a successful life, you will have to appropriately deal with the little foxes in your life. Self-examination and honesty will help you do this. What are the little foxes that are spoiling your vineyard?

List the little foxes that are wreaking havoc in your life. Then determine what steps you need to take to eliminate them from your life.

1. ______________________________
____

2. ______________________________
____

3. ______________________________
____

4. ______________________________
____

35.)

LEAP OR STEP?

The steps of a good man are ordered by the LORD and he delighteth in his way.
Psalm 37:23, KJV

We've defined success as fulfilling the purpose God has designed us for. Fortunately, Psalm 37:23 tells us that we don't have to figure out that purpose on our own. God will reveal it to us one step at a time. Let me reiterate—one step at a time!

Growing up in the charismatic movement, I saw many Christians talk about taking gigantic leaps of faith, so much so that I thought this concept was a biblical principle. I have to admit, I have taken a few leaps myself, and the outcome was not pretty. I laugh about it now, but I wasn't laughing then.

Nowhere in the Bible will you find the Christian life compared to a leap of faith. What the Bible does compare the Christian life to is a walk. Second Corinthians 5:7 tells us:

For we walk by faith, not by sight. (KJV)

Sometimes in the church, we can get the impression that the walk of faith is this mysterious and unpredictable process that really has no rhyme or reason. You may have heard someone talk about going "where the Spirit leads," as if the Spirit aimlessly leads us around. Is this really what walking by faith looks like?

Let's compare the walk of faith to a walk you might take with a friend down a path.

1. Take one step at a time. You put one foot in front of the other. So, too, when you walk by faith, you take one step at a time. None of this taking a leap into the great unknown! Many times God will give us directions only for the step immediately before us. Then, after we have obeyed Him in that area, He gives the next step. If you are having a hard time figuring out what your next step is, ask yourself if you have obeyed Him in His last instruction.
2. Make sure your footing is secure. When you take a step, you put your foot down on an object that can support you. If your footing is shaky, you redirect your step until you find a secure object to support your weight. Our walk with Christ works the same way. We complete the step that is immediately before us. Then we look to take the next step directly in front of us. If in the process we realize that our footing is not secure, we back off and redirect our step to the place where our footing is secure.
3. Getting from point A to point B takes many steps. Think about a simple walk from your front door to the end of your driveway. You do not get upset after taking one step out the door because you have not yet reached

your destination. Although the destination is only a short distance away, there are still many steps required. The walk of faith consists of many small steps. Don't get discouraged by all these steps.

4. Walking in faith also implies that we believe God's Word and choose to align our lives by the principles in His Word. As we've discussed earlier, this results in living a successful life.

The walk of faith is a lifelong journey. With each step of faith we take, the more mature we become. So keep taking steps in your life regardless of how mundane they may seem, and don't be fooled by opportunities that promise unheard-of forward strides. You'll get to your final destination if you'll patiently take it one step at a time.

1. Are you walking in faith? ______________________

   ____

2. Are you allowing God to determine your steps, or are you planning your own course? ___________

   ____

36.)

THE ONES GOD HELPS

God resisteth the proud, and giveth grace to the humble.
1 Peter 5:5, KJV

Pride—to some degree, we all deal with it in our lives. To what degree is it a factor for you? Now I'm not talking about confidence or feeling good about yourself. Rather, I'm talking about selfish pride that inflates your own importance at the expense of others. God hates this kind of pride. It is what caused the devil to be thrown out of heaven, and it is what causes us to think that we can do it on our own, not needing to rely on God.

Some people reek of pride. You can see it on their countenance, hear it in their voice, read it in their body language. It is easy to detect. But did you know that even the most humble person sometimes deals with pride? That is because at the root of every sin is pride. Pride tells us that we don't need to obey God. It gives us a false sense of self-sufficiency and ultimately cuts us off from God's help, because we think we don't need His help.

If you struggle with pride, repentance is just a prayer away. One of the Bible's most awesome examples of a repentant heart is that of King David.

We can read about his moral failure in 2 Samuel 11. After having an adulterous relationship in which a child was conceived, he had the woman's husband killed. The prophet Nathan confronted David, and immediately David repented. Even with that big blot against him, David was called a man after God's own heart.

We get a sense of David's repentant heart and his humility in Psalm 51. I remember being a senior in high school and my pastor talking about this psalm in one of his sermons. He told the congregation that if we ever felt as if we had committed the unpardonable sin or simply needed God to forgive us, we should pray Psalm 51. I have used this psalm as a prayer of repentance ever since, and I encourage you to do the same. As you read this psalm, make it your prayer. This is the starting point of true success:

Have mercy on me, O God,
according to your unfailing love;
according to your great compassion
blot out my transgressions.
Wash away all my iniquity
and cleanse me from my sin.
For I know my transgressions,
and my sin is always before me.
Against you, you only, have I sinned
and done what is evil in your sight,
so that you are proved right when you speak
and justified when you judge.

Surely I was sinful at birth,
sinful from the time my mother
conceived me.

Surely you desire truth in the inner parts;
you teach me wisdom in the inmost place.
Cleanse me with hyssop, and I will be clean;
wash me, and I will be whiter than snow.
Let me hear joy and gladness;
let the bones you have crushed rejoice.
Hide your face from my sins
and blot out all my iniquity.
Create in me a pure heart, O God,
and renew a steadfast spirit within me.
Do not cast me from your presence
or take your Holy Spirit from me.
Restore to me the joy of your salvation
and grant me a willing spirit, to sustain me.
Then I will teach transgressors your ways,
and sinners will turn back to you.
Save me from bloodguilt, O God,
the God who saves me,
and my tongue will sing of your
righteousness.
O Lord, open my lips,
and my mouth will declare your praise.
You do not delight in sacrifice,
or I would bring it;
you do not take pleasure in burnt offerings.
The sacrifices of God are a broken spirit;
a broken and contrite heart,
O God, you will not despise.
In your good pleasure make Zion prosper;
build up the walls of Jerusalem.
Then there will be righteous sacrifices,
whole burnt offerings to delight you;
then bulls will be offered on your altar.
(NIV 1984)

1. Is pride an issue for you? ____________________
____
____

2. What are some practical ways you could humble yourself? ______________________________
____
____

37.)

THE ULTIMATE EXTREME MAKEOVER

PART 1: SPIRIT

Therefore, if anyone is in Christ, the new creation has come: The old has gone, the new is here!
2 Corinthians 5:17

Have you ever watched an extreme makeover, whether it was a makeover of a family's home or of a person's physical body? The results are pretty dramatic. But what would the ultimate extreme makeover look like, the kind of makeover that could change a person's innermost core? Is it even possible, and if so, who can give such a makeover?

No doubt you have heard the phrase "God helps those who help themselves." I've heard people who have supported this statement, and I've also heard people who opposed such a concept. So who is right? In the case of providing the ultimate extreme makeover to the human heart, is it possible for any person to do this on his or her own, or is this kind of transformation dependent on God?

I suppose you could argue the point that there is a part we play and that God's hands are tied if we won't cooperate. On the flip side, you could argue that it is only by God's grace that we exist and that we are desperately reliant on Him.

Which side are you on? I guess I would have to agree with both sides. First of all, we have nothing and are nothing without God in our lives. But on the other hand, the Bible is full of commands that we are instructed to follow, so there is obviously a part for us to play. This is where the waters get murky: knowing what part is God's responsibility and adopting a hands-off policy in that department *and* knowing what part is ours and not expecting God to intervene.

Our walk with Christ is a partnership. It's similar to a contract. The Bible calls this contract a "covenant." In this covenant, both sides agree to the terms set forth in the agreement. God promises to fulfill His part, and we promise to fulfill our part.

If we don't understand the terms of the covenant, however, it's difficult, if not impossible, to abide by its terms. Many Christians do not understand the terms because they don't understand how God created man and what is expected of him in this covenant. So let's take a look at how God created us. Without this understanding, it will be impossible to live a successful and victorious Christian life, but with it we will understand what God's responsibility is as well as our responsibility in this covenant relationship.

The Bible says in 1 Thessalonians 5:23 that we are a three-part being: spirit, soul, and body.

May God himself, the God of peace, sanctify you through and through. May your whole spirit, soul and body be kept blameless at the coming of our Lord Jesus Christ.

We are going to look at each of these dimensions in separate chapters. The one we will focus on in this chapter is the spirit.

The spirit is the part of you that connects and communes with God. In our politically correct society, we are told that there are many ways for us to get to God; but the Bible makes it clear that there is only one way to God, and that is through His Son, Jesus Christ. Jesus Himself said:

I am the way and the truth and the life. No one comes to the Father, but by me.
John 14:6

Also, First Timothy 2:5 says:

For there is one God and one mediator between God and mankind, the man Christ Jesus.

According to the Bible, in order to come to God, we must go through Christ. This is what we call being a Christian, becoming a believer, or being saved. John 3:3 calls it being "born again," or numerous times throughout the New Testament, it is referred to as being "in Christ." When we are placed in Christ, an amazing thing happens: we get new hearts and new spirits.

I will give you a new heart and put a new spirit in you; I will remove from you your heart of stone and give you a heart of flesh. And I will put my Spirit in you and move you to follow my decrees and be careful to keep my law.
Ezekiel 36:26–27

Not only are you placed in Christ, but Christ is also in you. Colossians 1:27 says:

To them God has chosen to make known among the Gentiles the glorious riches of this mystery, which is Christ in you, the hope of glory.

It is as if Christ is a glass pitcher of clean, fresh water, and you are a glass of dirty, impure water. The glass represents your heart and your spirit before you come to Christ. We are told in Jeremiah 17:9:

The heart is deceitful above all things, and desperately wicked: who can know it? (KJV)

Psalm 14:3 tells us:

All have turned away, all have become corrupt; there is no one who does good, not even one.

So before you come to Christ, you are filthy and polluted, but when you surrender your life to the Lord Jesus Christ, your dirty glass of water is emptied, and Christ pours His pure, living water into your glass. Your spirit is infused with God's Spirit. It's as though you are getting God's DNA.

But it doesn't stop there. You are then placed in the pitcher of water, which represents Christ, and you are sealed with the Holy Spirit. Ephesians 1:13 says:

And you also were included in Christ when you heard the message of truth, the gospel of your salvation. When you believed, you were marked in him with a seal, the promised Holy Spirit.

If you know anything about canning food, you know that a very important step in the process is sealing the lid. Without the proper sealing, the contents of the jar will spoil, and your efforts will have been in vain. The seal keeps the good stuff in and the bad stuff out.

This is the picture we are given of the Holy Spirit in our conversion experience. It's as if the Holy Spirit acts like the lid that seals in the Spirit of God inside of us. Receiving Christ and being marked by the Holy Spirit with a seal is a one-time deal. There is never a need for you to get a new spirit, because your spirit is perfect. It will never lead you into temptation or sin. In fact, the Spirit of God Himself is living on the inside of you. You could say that once you receive Christ, the deal is signed, sealed, and delivered. It's a done deal.

Whose responsibility is it to give you a new spirit and seal you with the Holy Spirit? It's God's responsibility. The only part you play is confessing Jesus with your mouth and believing that

God raised Him from the dead (Romans 10:9–10; see chapter 1). This is the completion of Part 1.

RECAP: Getting a new Spirit and a new heart—God's responsibility

> If you have not yet experienced getting a new spirit and a new heart, today is your day! See chapter 1, "The Two Deal Breakers."

38.)

THE ULTIMATE EXTREME MAKEOVER

PART 2: SOUL

The law of the Lord is perfect, refreshing the soul. The statutes of the Lord are trustworthy, making wise the simple.
Psalm 19:7

We are continuing our discussion of the ultimate extreme makeover and established in the last chapter that when you come to Christ, you get a new spirit. But what about your soul, which consists of your mind, your will, and your emotions? Do you get a new one? The answer is no. Romans 12:2 tells you what you are to do with your soul.

Do not conform any longer to the pattern of this world, but be transformed by the renewing of your mind. Then you will be able to test and approve what God's will is—his good, pleasing and perfect will.

This is a great scripture, but it contains a lot of Bible lingo, so what exactly is it saying? First of all, when it tells us not to conform to the pattern of this world, it is essentially saying that we need to stop acting as the world acts. Can your coworkers, family, the cashier at the store, and all the people you deal with on a daily basis tell that you are different from non-Christians? Or is your behavior so similar that people can't tell the difference between you and them?

Is your mind renewed? Translation: Have you changed your thinking by meditating on (thinking over and over) God's Word? Or are you following the pattern of the world?

Before we come to Christ, we each have a certain way in which we deal with the world, ourselves, situations, and other people. It is our learned response. For example, in crisis situations, some people turn to cigarettes, others turn to money, and others may turn to alcohol. These kinds of patterns have been deeply ingrained in our thinking. They are just automatic responses. We don't even have to think about them.

Then, when we come to Christ, we are given a new spirit, but no one has hit the reset button on our soul. Instead, we have the responsibility to renew our mind by meditating on God's Word. As we begin to think about God's Word on a consistent basis, we begin to see our behavior change.

This is what the Bible means by being transformed by the renewing of your mind. It is a daily process, and it is your responsibility. If you're not meditating on God's Word, begin doing so today. This step is your responsibility. In the next chapter, we will finish the "Ultimate Extreme Makeover" as we talk about the third part of our being: the flesh.

1. Does a successful and victorious Christian life seem out of reach? ______________________________
____

2. Do you feel as if you're at the mercy of bad habits, addictions, or sins that you just can't seem to beat?
____
____

3. Do you see yourself as a sinner and not a saint?
____
______________________________Understand that renewing your mind takes time. There is no "Easy" button to push. The more you put God's Word in your heart, however, the more your behavior will conform to the Word, so don't give up! Regardless of how long it takes, if you keep at it, eventually you'll see change!

39.)

THE ULTIMATE EXREME MAKEOVER

PART 3: FLESH

Those who belong to Christ Jesus have crucified the flesh with its passions and desires.
Galatians 5:24

In the previous two chapters, we saw that as a three-part entity, we each have a spirit, which is made new when we come to Christ, and we each have a soul, which we must renew. Lastly, we each live in a physical body while we are on earth that the Bible refers to as "the flesh."

What is our relationship with the flesh? The Bible gives us only one action to take with our flesh. Crucify it! Romans 8:13 says:

For if you live according to [the dictates of] the flesh, you will surely die. But if through the power of the [Holy] Spirit you are [habitually] putting to death (making extinct, deadening) the [evil] deeds prompted by the body, you shall [really and genuinely] live forever.
(AMP)

Ephesians 4:22–24 says:

You were taught, with regard to your former way of life, to put off your old self, which is being corrupted by its deceitful desires; to be made new in the attitude of your minds; and to put on the new self, created to be like God in true righteousness and holiness.

Colossians 3:5–10 says:

Put to death, therefore, whatever belongs to your earthly nature: sexual immorality, impurity, lust, evil desires and greed, which is idolatry. Because of these, the wrath of God is coming. You used to walk in these ways, in the life you once lived. But now you must also rid yourselves of all such things as these: anger, rage, malice, slander, and filthy language from your lips. Do not lie to each other, since you have taken off your old self with its practices and have put on the new self, which is being renewed in knowledge in the image of its Creator.

This is where Christians get derailed. They think that just because they have a new spirit, they do not have to deal with their flesh. They don't understand how they have been created, that they have a body of flesh that has the law of sin and death operating in it.

It's easy to think that once you come to Christ, you don't have to deal with your flesh, but nothing could be further from the truth. Either you deal with your flesh or your flesh will deal with you.

Sadly, we have all seen examples of Christian leaders who have had moral failures, not just in front of their congregations, but in front of the entire world. They did great damage to the body of Christ because they refused to deal with their flesh, and eventually it took them over the edge.

That is the thing you have to realize. Your flesh will eventually take you over the edge if you do not subdue it. Many people like to get as close as they can to temptation. They like the thrill of playing with fire. But you can be sure that your flesh unchecked will always take you overboard—always. For this reason, we are told in Philippians 3:3 to put *no* confidence in the flesh.

For it is we who are the circumcision, we who serve God by his Spirit, who boast in Christ Jesus, and who put no confidence in the flesh.

One of my friends dealt with a terrible addiction, but by the grace of God, she had an incredible transformation and God totally restored her life. However, a few years later, she got into a business where she was constantly around that addiction. She was putting confidence in her flesh. I have not talked to her about the situation, but my guess is she is thinking something along the lines of "I now have the self-control to say no," or "I can handle it this time around." But however she justifies it, she is putting confidence in her flesh, and if left unchecked, it will lead her back to where she promised she would never go.

What does it look like, not putting any confidence in your flesh? Simply put, don't trust your flesh. The Bible calls it crucifying your flesh, and it involves setting yourself up for success by eliminating any and all situations that would take you down the path towards your temptation.

Hebrews 12:1 talks about the sin that so easily entangles. It's different for all of us. What is the sin that so easily entangles you? Avoid it at all costs. Create an environment where it is impossible to fail. If your struggle is with alcohol, arrange your life so that you are never around it. Avoid those things that bring temptation and increase the chance of your giving in to it, things such as television, people, situations, and events.

A great way to deal with the flesh can be seen in Galatians 5:16, which tells us that if we walk in the Spirit, we will not gratify the desires of the flesh. My chapter entitled " The Teeter-Totter" (chapter 11) talks about this very subject. When we crucify our flesh, we are living in line with the person that God created us to be.

My three-year-old provides yet another great analogy. There are times when she is rude or acts inappropriately, and my husband, Scott, will say, "Sophie, you're a Coates, and Coates don't act like that." He is not rejecting her or disowning her; rather, he is telling her that her behavior is not compatible with who she is. This is precisely what God says to us. He lovingly rebukes us, saying, "You're My child, and you have My DNA inside of you. Your behavior is not compatible with who you are."

How's your behavior? Are you dealing with your flesh, or is your flesh totally running all over you? I like to compare the flesh to a toddler, as you have probably noticed. If you have been around children this age for any amount of time, you know that at times you cannot reason with them at all. They can be totally irrational, fickle, and unwilling to cooperate. If they were left in charge, there would be no bedtime and no restrictions on television, sweets, pop, or anything else, for that matter.

When Sophie was two and a half, we moved from one part of town to another. Because of the many changes, we got into some not-so-good sleeping habits. After the move, Sophie went from sleeping in a crib to sleeping in a toddler bed. When it came time for her to go to bed, she would want either Scott or me to go to bed with her, so one of us would climb in bed with her and curl up in a little ball, which was the only way we could fit in her bed. At the time, this seemed like a minor inconvenience, so every night one of us would lie down with her until she fell asleep five or ten minutes later. As time went by, the five to ten minutes turned into forty-five minutes, and even then she might not be asleep. As soon as we would get up, she would insist that we get back in bed.

We finally decided enough was enough, and boy, it was not easy. The first few nights, she screamed—not just cried—for forty-five minutes before she finally fell asleep. It was painful, but we knew we had to follow through on our decision. Within just a few days, Sophie figured out that she was going to bed alone, and bedtimes became very uneventful. Now, not quite a year later, Sophie will at times try to use the diversion tactic to extend her bedtime, but by and large, once we tuck her into bed, we don't hear a peep out of her until morning.

Did you know that your flesh is a lot like a toddler? It will throw a fit, kick and scream, but as soon as it realizes you mean business, it will simmer down and cooperate. When you first tell your flesh it is not going to have its way any longer, it will protest, but eventually it will get the picture that you are serious.

Let's say, for example, that you are going to start waking up early every morning to spend time with God by reading the Bible and praying. Your flesh will most likely rebel, unless you're a morning person, and when the alarm clock goes off, your flesh will be screaming for you to hit the snooze button. However, if you're consistent, it won't be long until your flesh will fall in line. It might not like it, but it will understand there's no use in fighting.

We all deal with the flesh. It may be in different areas and on different levels, but every one of us has areas in which our flesh wants to dictate its will over us. The only way to subdue it is to crucify it, and this must be done daily.

Crucifying the flesh is our responsibility. Jesus has made a way for us to live above the impulses of our flesh. Are you crucifying your flesh?

Crucifying the flesh is something that we are to do daily. Are you crucifying your flesh, or do you let it do whatever it wants to do?

40.)

THE UMPIRE

Let the peace of Christ rule in your hearts, since as members of one body you were called to peace. And be thankful.
Colossians 3:15

One of the best pieces of advice I have ever received is to "always follow peace." What exactly is peace? According to *Webster's Dictionary*, peace can be defined as the following: "1: a state of tranquility or quiet; 2: freedom from disquieting or oppressive thoughts or emotions; 3: harmony in personal relations."[3]

Colossians 3:15 makes an interesting analogy. Take a look:

And let the peace (soul harmony which comes) from Christ rule (act as umpire continually) in your hearts [deciding and settling with finality all questions that arise in your minds, in that peaceful state] to which as [members of Christ's] one body you were also called [to live]. And be thankful (appreciative), [giving praise to God always]. (AMP)

In this scripture, peace is compared to an umpire. Think about the role an umpire plays in a baseball game. He or she determines which balls are in and which balls are out, among other things. Peace is like that umpire. It determines which choices are in and which ones are out. As you are contemplating a decision, peace will direct you in the way you should go.

Peace is a funny thing. You can have it in the most unlikely situations. And there are other times when you think you should have peace but it is nowhere to be found. That is your cue that you need to abort that plan and continue looking for the direction that peace is leading you. Always follow peace.

Not only does peace act as an umpire, but according to Philippians 4:7, it also acts as a guardian:

And the peace of God, which transcends all understanding, will guard your hearts and your minds in Christ Jesus.

Even when the winds of trial and tribulation are blowing, you can still experience peace. So what's the practical application here? How do you follow peace? When you have the Spirit of God living in your life, you have a direct line to God. The Bible talks about your spirit bearing witness with God's Spirit, which simply means that God speaks to your spirit and you just know what to do.

Living in peace is part of your God-given purpose. It is part of living a successful life. Is the peace of God ruling your heart? Are you following peace? Why not give up the worry and turmoil today? It's a decision you will never regret.

1. Is your life marked with peace? ________________
____

2. Do you have the sense that you are headed in the right direction? ______________________________
____

41.)

CHILL!

For we do not have a high priest who is unable to sympathize with our weaknesses, but we have one who has been tempted in every way, just as we are—yet he did not sin. Let us then approach God's throne of grace with confidence, so that we may receive mercy and find grace to help us in our time of need.

Hebrews 4:15–16

If you are one of those people who beat yourself up over a mistake, have an all-or-nothing mind-set, or take life too seriously, this chapter is for you. We all make mistakes. We all let ourselves and others down from time to time, but everyone deals with these mistakes differently. For some, it's no big deal. Life is a big party, and why waste any time regretting what you can't change? But then there are those of us who have a hard time rebounding after a shortcoming, so much so that we waste precious time making a mountain out of a molehill. If this scenario doesn't describe you, you can move on to the next chapter, but if you are like me, read on.

It was in college that I really began to have a problem in this area (or maybe it was in college where it was finally revealed). One of my best friends, Sherrie, would frequently tell me, "Give yourself a break!" She lived a couple of doors down from me during my freshman year of college and observed my destructive behavior of beating myself up over everything, from bombing a test to not achieving my goals, to basically not being perfect. Over the course of our friendship, she has told me frequently, "Give yourself a break!"

I think I can say this inability to deal with my mistakes was one of the biggest deterrents, if not the biggest, in keeping me from making forward progress. Sometimes you just have to roll with the punches and realize it is what it is and just move on, smarter and wiser. Chalk it up to the learning curve that just got smaller.

This was something that was extremely difficult for me to do. I wanted everything perfect. It was all or nothing, and I would not settle for anything less! The funny thing is that the more I expected perfection from myself, the more failure I encountered. Ironic.

Call it Type A personality or whatever you want, but why is it that some of us have a tougher time at this than others? I'm not sure, but I think it might be due to pride—pride that insists we are the master of our own fate; pride that tells us we are better, smarter, stronger—you fill in the blank—than we really are. But in the end, are we getting what we really want? I can't speak for everyone, but I'm guessing most people are like me and desire fulfillment, happiness, success, and a sense of purpose. From my experience, beating myself up didn't get me anywhere close to reaching those objectives.

Maybe you have never let up on yourself. Maybe you think that would make you weak, undisciplined, or lazy. It requires humbling yourself and admitting you aren't "all that." I'm not talking about being irresponsible, not working hard, and not having high expectations, but I am talking precisely about what Hebrews 4:16 describes. See if it's not what you are really looking for:

- Ability to draw near to the throne of grace (God's unmerited favor)
- Mercy for your failures
- Appropriate, well-timed help coming just when you need it

I'll take them all, thank you very much! It's time to chill!

1. Are you a perfectionist? ______________________________
____

2. Can you let go of the control and ask God for help?
____
____

3. Can you let up on yourself and give yourself a break?
____
____

42.)

INSANITY

Insanity is doing the same thing over and over again and expecting a different result.

Albert Einstein

In the first college counseling class I took, I remember hearing the professor say something along the lines of the above quote. Since that time, I've heard it repeated many times. I know it sounds obvious, but how many people do you know who have not figured that out? Maybe you're one of them.

I know I can say, "Been there, done that." In those moments, life was frustrating. Living a fulfilling and successful life seemed a million miles away, all because I didn't understand this principle. Fortunately, with time I learned this lesson and was able to make the necessary adjustments. It's very liberating to know that at any time you can make a different choice and change the direction of your life.

Where are you in regards to making changes in your life? Do you need to stop the insanity? Take a quick assessment of your life, and take note of the areas that you are trying to change by doing the same thing:

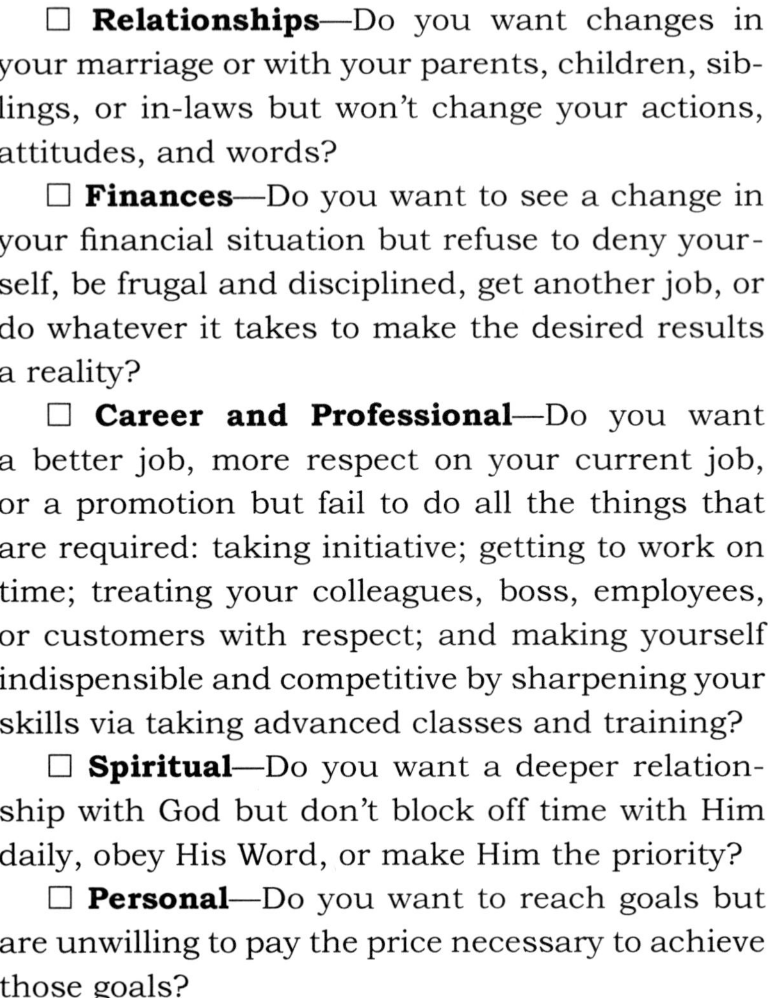

☐ **Relationships**—Do you want changes in your marriage or with your parents, children, siblings, or in-laws but won't change your actions, attitudes, and words?

☐ **Finances**—Do you want to see a change in your financial situation but refuse to deny yourself, be frugal and disciplined, get another job, or do whatever it takes to make the desired results a reality?

☐ **Career and Professional**—Do you want a better job, more respect on your current job, or a promotion but fail to do all the things that are required: taking initiative; getting to work on time; treating your colleagues, boss, employees, or customers with respect; and making yourself indispensible and competitive by sharpening your skills via taking advanced classes and training?

☐ **Spiritual**—Do you want a deeper relationship with God but don't block off time with Him daily, obey His Word, or make Him the priority?

☐ **Personal**—Do you want to reach goals but are unwilling to pay the price necessary to achieve those goals?

If you have been trying to make changes but just can't seem to get the job done, ask yourself if you are doing the same miserable thing over and over, hoping for different results. It may be that making some changes will take you from insanity to successfully accomplishing your goals.

STOP THE INSANITY!

Take some time to reflect on your life. In what areas are you doing the same thing over and over and seeing negative results but keep expecting different results?

1. ______________________________

____

2. ______________________________

____

3. ______________________________

____

Now determine what changes you are going to make for the above:

1. ______________________________

____

2. ______________________________

____

3. ______________________________

____

43.)

AMAZING GRACE

For out of His fullness (abundance) we have all received [all had a share and we were all supplied with] one grace after another and spiritual blessing upon spiritual blessing and even favor upon favor and gift [heaped] upon gift.
John 1:16, AMP

Grace. It truly is amazing. The Amplified Bible describes it as the "unmerited favor of God." When you have grace, everything just goes more smoothly. Grace doesn't remove the responsibility, hard work, endurance, or challenges; it just makes it easier to get through them and leads you to success. Your life is characterized by peace, joy, and fulfillment.

Contrast that with the opposite: no grace. When there is no grace present, you definitely know it. Life is a drag. Things are tough. There's just no flow. You are out of sync. It feels as if you are banging your head on the wall.

One thing I have learned is that living with grace is awesome, but living without it stinks. Talk about defeat! That is why I have endeavored to do only those things where God's grace dwells. That may sound like a cop-out, an excuse to do only things that are pleasant, but that is not the case at all. I'll give you an example.

When I interviewed for my first teaching job, I knew exactly the size of the school I wanted to teach at, the classes I wanted to teach, and the sports I wanted to coach. I attended a teachers' job fair and interviewed with nine different schools. Of those schools, there were two that I was really interested in teaching at. However, one of the schools that called me back for a second interview was Chanute High School in Chanute, Kansas.

I was definitely not interested in moving to Chanute. It was a much larger school than what I wanted to teach in, and the position open would require that I teach physical science and biology to freshmen and sophomores. I wanted to teach chemistry to juniors and seniors. So when the principal's secretary called me for a second interview, I politely declined. But they would not take no for an answer. After much persistence on their part, I finally relented, especially after their offer to pay for my gas to get there.

I just knew that this would not be the place for me. However, everything changed the moment that I stepped on campus. I had such favor with everyone I met. There was such a grace and a peace that when I left six hours later, I knew this was the place for me. What changed? Not my prerequisites. I still would be teaching in a high school of about 650 students, and I would still be teaching freshmen and sophomores, not juniors and seniors.

It turns out the grace I had there was amazing. I had many great opportunities and experiences, as well as developed many great relationships. When I felt the grace was gone about five years later, that's when I knew it was time for me to move on.

Are you experiencing God's grace in your life? Either you have it or you don't. Know this: if you are not currently walking in grace, there is a place where grace exists. Your job is to find it and get there. It's amazing. Don't miss out on it another moment.

Are you living in grace? Answer the following questions to help you in your quest for peace.

1. Do I have peace in my life? ______________________
____
____

2. Do I sense an ease in what I am doing, or am I constantly frustrated? ______________________
____
____

3. Do I have a knowing in my heart that I am right where I need to be? ______________________
____
____

44.)

CATAPULT

Instead of your [former] shame you shall have a twofold recompense; instead of dishonor and reproach [your people] shall rejoice in their portion. Therefore in their land they shall possess double [what they had forfeited]; everlasting joy shall be theirs.
Isaiah 61:7, AMP

It's one thing you can count on in this life: you're going to have trouble. In fact, the Bible guarantees it. What a bummer! But hold it. What if those troubles can serve to make you stronger, wiser, and better prepared for life's challenges? What if those troubles can be used as a springboard that catapults you to greater victory, greater success, and greater glory?

"How is that possible?" you may ask. The Bible says that we go from glory to glory. So if we are guaranteed to have troubles (which we are) but are told that we go from glory to glory, obviously those troubles can result in God's glory being revealed in our lives.

What is glory anyway? According to the Amplified Bible, *glory* is the "manifested goodness of God." When troubles come our way, it is God's desire to use those troubles to showcase His goodness in us. Basically, He wants to make us more like Him.

Maybe that isn't all that encouraging to you when you are in the midst of trouble, but this should be:

And we know that in all things God works for the good of those who love him, who have been called according to his purpose.
Romans 8:28

Note that it does not say that all things are good; rather, it says God can work everything out for our good. There are things that come our way that are bad; they are not God's will, and they steal, kill, and destroy. But God in His sovereignty has the capability to turn those circumstances around for our good.

When we place our trust in God, even our troubles can be turned around for our benefit. Are you allowing God to use your troubles to your advantage?

1. In what areas of your life have you experienced loss or defeat? ______________________________
____
____

2. What things in your past would you change if you could? ______________________________
____
____

God wants to turn these things around for your benefit. Give them to God and trust Him to work all things for your good.

45.)

WHATEVER YOU DO, DON'T QUIT

Let us not become weary in doing good, for at the proper time we will reap a harvest if we do not give up.
Galatians 6:9

This chapter may appear to be for those at the end of their rope, ready to give up. Although it is for those folks, it really applies to all of us. Are you ready to call it quits in any of the following areas?

- Your marriage
- Your pursuit of a strong relationship with a family member, friend, spouse, or child
- Your dream
- Your faith
- Your search for purpose and meaning instead of living the status quo
- The thing you feel passionate about and are called to do
- Your previous commitments
- Your pursuit of a healthy lifestyle, eating healthy and exercising
- Your pursuit of freedom over an addiction
- Your pursuit of trying to do the right thing

- Your pursuit of kicking a bad habit once and for all

Perseverance can be exhausting. It takes grit and tenacity to keep going when everything inside you is screaming to bail. Sometimes pressing through a difficult situation or challenge can take years, involve lots of sweat and tears, and require that you choose commitment over convenience. And who wants to do that?

In James 1:2, we are told to "consider it pure joy whenever you face trials of many kinds." I can think of a lot of things that give me pure joy, but facing trials is not one that comes to mind. Pure joy is hearing my baby laugh, watching a beautiful sunset, hearing my three-year-old sing, hanging out with my family and friends, driving through the countryside in summer to look at cornfields. How could you possibly place facing trials in the same category? It's possible because enduring a hard time produces perseverance that results in becoming mature and complete, not lacking anything. Not a bad end result, wouldn't you say?

Here's my secret for not quitting; maybe it will help you: settle it once and for all that quitting is not an option. There have been challenges in my life in which it seemed I would never see victory. Yes, I was tempted to quit, but I knew in my heart that God was saying to keep at it and not give up. Some of these challenges I faced for years. For me, the real victory came, not when I got the breakthrough, but when I finally said to God, myself, and the devil, "I'm not quitting. I may go to my grave pursuing the assignment God gave me, but I'm not quitting. Period. End of discussion."

The choice was made and the issue settled. Is it time for you to make your choice and settle your issue once and for all? Let James 1:2–5 be a source of encouragement:

Consider it pure joy, my brothers and sisters, whenever you face trials of many kinds, because you know that the testing of your faith produces perseverance. Let perseverance finish its work so that you may be mature and complete, not lacking anything. If any of you lacks wisdom, you should ask God, who gives generously to all without finding fault, and it will be given to you.

> Do you need to make a commitment once and for all that you will finish your assignment?

46.)

WHAT IS PROSPERITY ANYWAY?

Beloved, I pray that you may prosper in every way and [that your body] may keep well, even as [I know] your soul keeps well and prospers.
3 John 1:2, AMP

Did you know that God wants you not only to be successful but also to prosper? I'm not referring to some excessive and indulgent prosperity that we hear a flaky evangelist talk about on television. We all have heard the promises of vast wealth, which include driving an expensive car, living in a luxurious house, and taking lavish vacations. But God's promise of prosperity transcends the wealth of the rich and famous we are so familiar with in America and other prosperous countries. It is about so much more than having a bunch of stuff.

Yes, God does want you to prosper financially. If you don't believe it, take a look at Galatians 3:29. It says we are Abraham's heirs. Part of that inheritance is spiritual blessing, but the blessing of Abraham goes beyond just spiritual blessing. Abraham was richly blessed financially as well. A little Old Testament study of Abraham's life will reveal he was very prosperous financially.

An argument I have heard many times is "What about people in Third World countries? How can you tell them they can be prosperous?" If that describes your thought process, you need to adjust your mind-set. Most likely you are equating prosperity (which is God's idea) with lots of money, nice cars, a big home, etc. (the world's idea). Is that true prosperity?

I don't subscribe to that definition at all. Prospering is about having all your needs met so that you can be generous with other people. All throughout the Bible, we are told to give and help others. If your needs aren't met, how can you help someone else? When you are prosperous, not only can you pay your electric bill, but you can also help the single mom living next door with her electric bill after she loses her job.

Get this! Prospering is not about having lots of money; it's about having more than you need, and that doesn't always involve money. In some cultures, having a wad of cash would be absolutely worthless, but having a bountiful crop of corn or rice would equal prosperity. For others, it would be having a cow or goat and a few chickens. Maybe what you currently need is not money, but a creative idea. Or maybe what you most need is a swift kick in the pants to get off the couch, stop being lazy, and get to work!

God wants to bless you and prosper you in your physical needs, but it doesn't stop there. Many of the people in our society that we would consider prosperous are bankrupt spiritually, relationally, and emotionally. Is a life without peace, joy, and freedom really prosperity? Is it really success?

When you look at the Bible's definition of prosperity, specifically 3 John 1:3, how would you rate your prosperity?

1. What do you think when you hear the word prosperity? Does it conjure up a negative image of excess, selfishness, greed, and extreme indulgence?

    ____

    ____

    ____

    ____

2. Remember that prosperity is God's idea. The world and the devil may have twisted it into a selfish, insatiable desire for personal gain, but that is not the original or authentic intent. When you think of prosperity in terms of God's definition, gaining so that you can be a blessing, a conduit of His grace, do you believe that He wants you to prosper?

    ____

    ____

    ____

    ____

47.)

SUCCESS IS ULTIMATELY ABOUT ETERNITY

It's not possible for a person to succeed—I'm talking about eternal success—without heaven's help.
John 3:27, MSG

Life is a vapor.

No matter what you do in this life, you have only a limited number of years. For some, that might be a hundred years, but when you consider the span of eternity, that really isn't very long. What really counts is where you will spend eternity and the kind of legacy you will leave behind.

Where will you spend eternity? What a waste to spend those hundred years or so on earth toiling, only to find yourself in eternal damnation. The Bible makes it clear that the way to heaven involves repenting of your sins and believing in Jesus Christ. Unfortunately, this is not the path that many people take. Matthew 7:13–14 says:

> ***Enter through the narrow gate. For wide is the gate and broad is the road that leads to destruction, and many enter through it. But small is the gate and narrow the road that leads to life, and only a few find it.***

What kind of legacy will you leave? Maybe you are on the path that leads to heaven, but are you leaving an eternal footprint? Are you spending your time with activities that will result in eternal rewards, or are they simply things that will fade away once your time here on earth has transpired?

The most important decision you will ever make involves where you will spend eternity. It's the fool that thinks he has plenty of time and can put off that decision for another day. Don't delay. It's the best decision you'll ever make. Period.

> If success is ultimately about the finale, the legacy of helping others you leave behind (aka eternity), would your life be a success or a failure if it ended now?
>
> ___
> ___
> ___
> ___

48.)

NEVER LET THEM SEE YOU SWEAT

But blessed are those who trust in the LORD and have made the LORD their hope and confidence.
Jeremiah 17:7, NLT

Not to show my age, but when I was growing up, there was an antiperspirant commercial on television that had the tag "Never let them see you sweat." The point was that even if you are frazzled on the inside, don't let it show on the outside. Confidence, in this case, is holding it together even when you feel you could crack.

Webster's Dictionary defines confidence as "1. a: a feeling of consciousness of one's powers or of one's reliance on circumstances; b: faith that one will act in a right, proper or effective way."[4]

Where does confidence originate? Some people are just naturally confident; for others, confidence may come from position, education, ability, social status, or from their financial situation. The climate in your family growing up is also going to play a role. You will likely be more confident if you grew up in a home that was encouraging and respectful, as well as one that placed a value on your individuality and uniqueness.

Where have you placed your confidence? Is it in your ability, your money, your looks, your knowledge, your skill, your pedigree, your position, or your talents? While those things aren't necessarily bad in themselves, the Bible instructs us not to place our confidence in them. Here's a look at where we are to place our confidence and where we are not to place our confidence.

Where to place your confidence:

For the LORD shall be your confidence and will keep your foot from being snared. Proverbs 3:26, NIV 1984

In him and through faith in him we may approach God with freedom and confidence. Ephesians 3:12

Where *not* to place your confidence:

For we [Christians] . . . put no confidence or dependence [on what we are] in the flesh and on outward privileges and physical advantages and external appearances. Philippians 3:3, AMP

God does want us to have confidence, but it is not confidence in ourselves. It is confidence in Him. We are told in Psalm 65:5 that He is:

the confidence and hope of all the ends of the earth. (AMP)

But when it comes to confidence found elsewhere, Isaiah 28:20 says:

All their sources of confidence will fail them. (AMP)

If your formula for confidence is in anything other than God, you are guaranteed failure. For success, choose the alternative: free access to God by placing your confidence in Him. Where is your confidence?

Ask yourself the following two questions:

1.) On a scale from 1 to 10, how confident am I?

____

2.) Where is my confidence: in my abilities or in God?

____

____

____

____

49.)

DILIGENCE

***Laziness makes a man poor,
but diligent hands bring wealth.***
Proverbs 10:4, NIV 1984

When it comes to success, I would be remiss if I didn't talk about the importance of having a good work ethic as well as the importance of being diligent. You really can't separate these qualities from success. In fact, doing a study on successful people will reveal they were relentless in their pursuit of their dream, whatever that dream may have been.

If you are thinking that your talent or resources will take you far and you don't plan to roll up your sleeves and get to work, you're kidding yourself. As I've said earlier, you reap what you sow. If you don't sow anything, you won't reap anything. So on your journey to success, don't forget the importance of good ol'- fashioned hard work.

Is your diligence and work ethic an asset or a liability?

1. Rate your diligence from 1 to 10.

   ____

   ____

2. Rate your work ethic from 1 to 10.

   ____

   ____

50.)

GOT SKILL?

Do you see someone skilled in their work? They will serve before kings; they will not serve before officials of low rank.
Proverbs 22:29

In our discussion of the real definition of success, it's apparent that God is a major player in the formula. Success, after all, was His idea. It may be easy to get the impression that this leaves us with little responsibility.

Although God is a big part of the equation, there is a part that we must play. God will not do it for us, and without our cooperation, success will not be realized.

One of those responsibilities is to be skilled at what we do. There are numerous scriptures in the Old Testament where God gave the children of Israel a job to do, such as constructing the temple, leading worship, or making garments for the tabernacle. Along with the assignment came the commission for skilled workers to do the job. God wanted the job to be done right.

Take a look at the following scriptures:

You have many workers: stonecutters, masons and carpenters, as well as those skilled in every kind of work in gold and

silver, bronze and iron—craftsmen beyond number. Now begin the work, and the Lord be with you.
1 Chronicles 22:15–16, emphasis added

The workers labored faithfully. . . . The Levites—all who were* skilled *in playing musical instruments.
2 Chronicles 34:12, emphasis added

Make the tabernacle with ten curtains of finely twisted linen and blue, purple and scarlet yarn, with cherubim woven into them by a* skilled *worker.
Exodus 26:1, emphasis added

God wanted quality and excellence back then, and He wants quality and excellence from us now. What does that mean for us? It may be that we go to school to take classes, become an apprentice, or get on-the-job training in a skill we want to learn. It may mean taking additional training or certification in our field.

Maybe you don't struggle professionally, but rather relationally. It could be that you need some people skills or communications skills. Or maybe what trips you up are your finances, and you need to learn skills in handling money. Whatever the issue, Ecclesiastes 10:10 contains a key principle regarding the relationship between skill and success. It says:

If the ax is dull and its edge unsharpened, more strength is needed, but skill will bring success.

If you are lacking success in any area, ask yourself what skills you need to learn to help you succeed. Then begin the process of learning those skills one step at a time. As you do, you will begin to make yourself marketable. You will find that you will become a valuable and desirable commodity, and you will become more successful because now you have a product to sell—yourself, a skillful worker.

1. In what areas are you lacking success? ________
____
____
____
____

2. What skills would bring you success? ________
____
____
____
____

3. What steps do you need to take to acquire those skills? ________________________________
____
____
____

51.)

WELCOME TO THE NEW NORMAL

But the fruit of the Spirit is love, joy, peace, patience, kindness, goodness, faithfulness, gentleness and self-control. Against such things there is no law.
Galatians 5:22-23, NIV 1984

What's your normal? Is it discord, turmoil, addictions, fear, bondage, uncontrolled thoughts, discouragement, or depression? Is it stress, anxiety, or loneliness? Imagine how your life would be if the following described you:

Love, joy, peace, patience, kindness, goodness, faithfulness, gentleness, and self-control

Wouldn't you agree that life would be really good if these descriptive words portrayed your "normal"? Would you consider your life a success if you possessed these qualities in great quantities?

These characteristics are what is referred to as "the fruit of the Spirit." That basically means they are the characteristics that are developed in your life as you remain in Christ by remaining in His Word. What does it mean to remain in the

Word? When we read the Bible and study it and then put it into practice, these characteristics are developed in our lives much as a piece of fruit is developed on a tree. For the believer, these characteristics are meant to be the norm.

If your life is chaotic and full of anything but the fruit described in Galatians, you can tap into the vine, Jesus, and begin bearing good fruit. John 15:5 says it this way:

I am the vine; you are the branches. If you remain in me and I in you, you will bear much fruit; apart from me you can do nothing.

Are you trying to bear good fruit without tapping into the vine? If so, it's useless. Fruit cannot be produced if the branches are cut off from the vine (tree).

As you take a look at your life, what is being produced: good fruit or bad fruit? If your answer is bad fruit, are you ready to move beyond the inner conflicts that plague your soul? Your new normal awaits you. What are you waiting for?

What's the fruit in your life?

1. Love or hate
2. Joy or sadness and woe
3. Peace or turmoil
4. Patience or impatience
5. Kindness or harshness
6. Goodness or ungraciousness
7. Faithfulness or unfaithfulness
8. Gentleness or abrasiveness
9. Self-control or lack of self-control

52.)
YOU GOT TO GET THIS

God is no respecter of persons.
Acts 10:34, KJV

Don't you just love God's sense of humor? Occasionally He will speak to me in a humorous way, and this lesson was one of those moments. I was cruising around Tulsa, just talking to God, when He began really speaking to my heart about this verse. I knew it was really important when He said, "You got to get this." There was an urgency to the point He was making.

A few moments later, a lady pulled out recklessly in traffic in her navy Bentley. She was driving as if she owned the road and wasn't what we would refer to as a "friendly driver." I watched her swerve in and out of traffic and refuse to let other vehicles pull in front of her. All the while, I had a big smile on my face.

God had just made a point, and here He was giving me the visual aid. God was no more impressed with this lady in her Bentley as He was with the person next to her in a clunker. I fell somewhere in between, driving my Dodge Caravan minivan.

It's easy for us to think people are important because of the positions they hold, the houses they live in, the cars they drive, the social circles they are part of, and the list goes on and on. However, these are not the things that impress God. In fact, He is probably amused when He sees how enamored we become with these trivial aspects of life.

What really impresses God is the heart. First Samuel 16:7 says:

People look at the outward appearance, but the Lord looks at the heart.

How would you like to impress God? I think you would agree that impressing God could be considered the definition of success. And when God is impressed with us, no doubt He is working on our behalf.

As you take a look at your life, are you well put together on the outside but lacking on the inside? Or maybe your heart is right, but your outward appearances are not that desirable. Remember, God is no respecter of persons. It's the heart that impresses Him. Is He impressed with yours?

1. How do you rate your importance as compared with others? ______________________________
____
____

2. How does your outward appearance compare with that of your heart? ______________________________
____
____

3. Do you spend more time focused on the outward appearance than you do on the inside? __________
____
____

53.)

GLOSSY IMITATION

This day I call the heavens and the earth as witnesses against you that I have set before you life and death, blessings and curses. Now choose life, so that you and your children may live.
Deuteronomy 30:19

Imagine that you and your family are going on a vacation to a tropical-island paradise. Your bags are packed, and you eagerly await the moment you will see the white or pink sand, turquoise water, and palm trees waving in the ocean breeze. To your dismay, as you arrive at the airport, you are told the airlines are on strike and you will not be able to take your vacation. However, to compensate you, the airlines have lined up rooms at a nearby hotel and have rented the ballroom, where they have placed life-sized placards with glossy images of the beach scenes you will be foregoing. This is your consolation.

Can you imagine how you would feel? Chances are you would be livid. And the reasons are obvious. A glossy imitation can't come close to the experience you would have in person on a tropical island: the warmth of the sun, the sand between your toes, and the beautiful scenery.

This scenario is similar to life, where we are presented with two options to attain success. One is a glossy imitation, and the other is the authentic version. God's version is the authentic one. Job 12:13–25 says:

Strength and success belong to God. (MSG)

However, if we don't know what authentic success is, we may pursue the glossy imitation and miss the real deal altogether.

The Bible contrasts success according to the world's standard with God's success. In regards to those who seek success according to the world's standards, Job 24:18–25 says:

They may get their brief successes,
but then it's over, nothing to show for it.
Like yesterday's newspaper, they're used
to wrap up the garbage. (MSG)

As you ponder which definition of success you are pursuing, I'll leave you with words from the wise King Solomon. He sums up our purpose and gives us the "end of the matter".

All has been heard; the end of the matter is: Fear God [revere and worship Him, knowing that He is] and keep His commandments, for this is the whole of man [the full, original purpose of his creation, the object of God's providence, the root of character, the foundation of all happiness, the adjustment to all inharmonious circumstances and conditions under the sun] and

the whole [duty] for every man. Ecclesiastes 12:13 (AMP)

When the last chapter of your life has been written will you have fulfilled your purpose, the real definition of success?

NOTES

WHO ARE YOU

1. Neil T. Anderson, *Victory Over The Darkness,* Ventura, (CA: Regal Books, 1990).

THE SUCCESS FORMULA

2. "Meditation," *Wikipedia, The Free Encyclopedia,* Wikimedia Foundation Inc., http://en.wikipedia.org/wiki/Meditation, (accessed February 18, 2012).

THE UMPIRE

3. "Peace," Merriam-Webster.com. 2012, http://www.merriam-webster.com/dictionary/peace, (accessed February 20, 2012).

NEVER LET THEM SEE YOU SWEAT

4. "Confidence," Merriam-Webster.com. 2012, http://www.merriam-webster.com/dictionary/confidence?show=0&t=1329793663, accessed February 20, 2012.

CPSIA information can be obtained at www.ICGtesting.com
Printed in the USA
LVOW132128080512

280799LV00002B/4/P